The Geography of Hope

A Tribute to Wallace Stegner

The Geography of Hope

Edited by Page Stegner
and Mary Stegner

Sierra Club Books   *San Francisco*

The Sierra Club, founded in 1892 by John Muir, has devoted itself to the study and protection of the earth's scenic and ecological resources—mountains, wetlands, woodlands, wild shores and rivers, deserts and plains. The publishing program of the Sierra Club offers books to the public as a nonprofit educational service in the hope that they may enlarge the public's understanding of the Club's basic concerns. The point of view expressed in each book, however, does not necessarily represent that of the Club. The Sierra Club has some sixty chapters coast to coast, in Canada, Hawaii, and Alaska. For information about how you may participate in its programs to preserve wilderness and the quality of life, please address inquiries to Sierra Club, 730 Polk Street, San Francisco, CA 94109.

The publisher gratefully acknowledges the generosity of the writers and photographers who donated their work to be included here. Many thanks to the periodicals in which some of the essays and photographs were previously published. All proceeds from the sale of this book will be donated to support the educational programs of the Sierra Club.

LIBRARY OF CONGRESS CATALOGING-IN-PUBLICATION DATA

Stegner, Page.
    The geography of hope : a tribute to Wallace Stegner / by Page and Mary Stegner.
        p.   cm.
    ISBN 0-87156-883-7 (pbk. : alk. paper)
    1. Stegner, Wallace Earle, 1909–1993. 2. Authors, American—20th century—Biography. 3. Western stories—History and criticism. 4. West (U.S.)—Historiography. 5. West (U.S.)—In literature. I. Stegner, Wallace Earle, 1909–1993. II. Stegner, Mary. III. Title.
PS3537.T316Z92   1996
813'.52—dc20
[B]   95-39025
                                                CIP

Production by Janet Vail
Book and cover design by James Robertson
Cover photograph by Chuck Painter
Composition by Wilsted & Taylor
Printed in the United States of America
10   9   8   7   6   5   4   3   2   1

Contents

Preface

When my father died of the injuries he sustained in an automobile wreck in Santa Fe, New Mexico, in 1993, there was not
only a tremendous expression of condolence and sympathy
to the immediate family but wide-spread media acknowledg-
ment of a great public loss. Lengthy tributes were paid to him
on National Public Radio, as well as on commercial and public
television stations around the country. There were remembrance
gatherings in locations as diverse as the U.S. Department of Interior in Washington, D.C., and Kepler's bookstore in Menlo Park,
California. Commemorations were held at the Memorial Church
Chapel at Stanford University in Palo Alto, the Buckley Center
Auditorium at the University of Portland, and the Herbst The-
ater in San Francisco. Symposiums to celebrate both his life
and work were organized at the Universities of Montana, New
Mexico, and Wisconsin. The University of Utah College of Law
named its Center for Land, Resources and the Environment in
his honor.

There were, in addition, a great number of personal tributes
written by other writers, some of them former students, some
close friends, some only slightly acquainted, but bonded by
"westernness" and a commonality of purpose in the stories
westerners have to tell. I do not know who first suggested that
these various expressions be gathered into a single volume, nor
do I remember at what point Barbara Ras at Sierra Club Books
persuaded me to act as its "coordinator," but reading through
one remarkable essay after another, it soon came to me that in
this editorial role I had been more honored than obligated.

All of us who have contributed to this volume offer it in tribute to the man who for many of us stood as a prime example of the will and discipline and depth of knowledge required to be a writer of great consequence—and of the generosity, personal integrity, inner strength, and compassion required to be a human being of any consequence. He was, as a number of writers in this volume have observed, an exemplum of character revealed through action, conducting himself in absolute accord with his fundamental belief in human dignity.

Looking at it from the vantage of one who had a closer opportunity to observe than most, I find it remarkable how consistently he appeared (and appears) to those who admired him —and how in keeping with my own experience the recollections of others are. In a sense, it seems, we were all his sons and daughters, uniformly treated by him in equal measures of affection and respect; treated not as acolytes, students, underlings, the less accomplished, but as peers. Because that, indeed, is how he essentially perceived us.

This is a book about Wallace Stegner, written by some of his friends and colleagues. Yet it has far greater resonance than a mere collection of memorial applause. It is a book about what one man has taught us, by his example, about the accountable life; a book about what it means to be a responsible, loving, thoughtful constituent of the human race. That is the only way he would have it.

Page Stegner
Santa Cruz, 1995

The Geography of Hope

His Finest Work of Art
Was Himself

Jackson J. Benson

WALLACE STEGNER DIED ON APRIL 13, 1993, in Santa Fe, New Mexico, as a result of injuries suffered in an auto accident two weeks earlier. During a long and distinguished career he received just about every award an American writer could, including a Pulitzer Prize for the 1971 novel, *Angle of Repose,* and a 1977 National Book Award for *The Spectator Bird.* Among his many other tributes was a PEN West Freedom to Write Award given to him last year to mark his refusal of the National Medal of Arts—which would have been presented by President Bush—in order to protest the politicization of the NEA. In accepting the PEN award, he wrote, "I believe that government should support the arts. I also believe that its function stops with support—it has no business trying to direct or censor them. Art must be left to the artists."

Born in Iowa, he spent his childhood on the last homestead frontier in Saskatchewan and the latter part of his life in the foothills of California. During his growing up, Stegner's father, a "boomer" looking to strike it rich, dragged the family from one place to another, finally settling down for a few years as a bootlegger in Salt Lake City. A big, strong, violent man who tried to pursue frontier values in a post-pioneer society, George Stegner became the basis for Bo Mason in *The Big Rock Candy Mountain* (1943), a novel which embodied the rootlessness, mobility, and rugged individualism that typified so much of western experience.

Physically weak as a child and scorned by his father, Wallace found acceptance in school and ended up working his way through the University of Utah and graduate school at the University of Iowa. He earned a Ph.D. in American literature and went on to teach at Utah, Wisconsin, Harvard, and Stanford. He was also a staff member for many years at the granddaddy of all the summer writing workshops, the Bread Loaf Writer's Conference in Vermont. It was there he met Robert Frost and Bernard DeVoto—who would become longtime friends and influence his work. During the 1940s and 1950s, he became known as an important short story writer. Nine of his stories would appear in volumes of the annual *Best American Short Stories*, and five in the *O. Henry Memorial Award Prize Stories*, including second prizes for "Two Rivers" (1942) and "Beyond the Glass Mountain" (1948) and a first prize for "The Blue-Winged Teal" (1954).

He was a man, to paraphrase Robert Stone, who practiced the virtues that most of us used to believe in—kindness, courtesy, responsibility, and hard work. He had many roles—novelist, essayist, historian, lecturer, editor, and environmentalist—but perhaps all of them go back to one central role, that of teacher. As teacher in the formal sense, he is known for founding the creative writing program at Stanford University, which he directed for twenty-five years, producing several dozen of our most accomplished writers. As teacher in a less formal sense, he was all his life a truth-seeker who tried to see himself, his history, his land, and his people as clearly as possible and pass on those discoveries to others.

As a westerner who frequently wrote about western subjects, he worked to increase our understanding of the West—its history, its geography, and its social dynamics—and to expose the myths that all too often have contributed to its exploitation. His Mormon histories displayed the fallacy of a West created by the lone horseman and demonstrated how important cooperation was to its actual development. His biography of John Wesley Powell performed the invaluable service of reminding us that the West was not a New Eden, a paradise, but for the most part an arid near desert. His biography of Bernard DeVoto did much to spread the DeVoto gospel concerning the need to preserve public lands and the need for constant public vigilance in their protection. With these latter two works alone, he made a substantial contribution to the emergence, development, and agenda of the environmental movement.

As an environmentalist, he was well known for his activities on behalf of the Sierra Club and the Wilderness Society, as well as for his many publications on the subject. Among these was the "Wilderness Letter" (1961), which defined wilderness as "the geography of hope": "Something will have gone out of us as a people if we ever let the remaining wilderness be destroyed; if we permit the last virgin forests to be turned into comic books and plastic cigarette cases; if we drive the few remaining members of the wild species into zoos or to extinction."

For those who knew Wallace Stegner personally, his loss is particularly difficult to bear. In a way, his finest work of art was himself—he often declared that his motive for writing was to examine himself, his roots, his motives and goals. Out of that self-examination, and a determination to grow, came one of the most remarkable persons of this or any other time. We in the West can take him, in death, to our hearts to cherish as one of ours, the best of what we can be. But we can also with some pride present him to the world, a great man and a great American writer.

The Quiet Revolutionary

James R. Hepworth

"I WOULD LIKE TO THINK that one life is enough," Wallace
Stegner told me once, "and that when I see it coming to an
end I can meet the darkness with resignation and perhaps
acceptance. I have been lucky. I came from nowhere, and
had no reason to expect as much from this one life as I have
got. I owe God a death, and the earth a pound or so of chemi-
cals. Now let's see if I can remember that when the time comes."

The time came on April 13, 1993, when Wallace Stegner died
in a hospital in Santa Fe, New Mexico, sixteen days after being
severely injured in a car wreck. He was 84 years old.

He left a legacy as writer, teacher, and conservationist that
once moved Edward Abbey to pronounce him "the only living
American worthy of the Nobel." Indeed, Stegner was one of the
American West's preeminent historians and arguably the most
important of its novelists. His work, unequaled in the American
literature of place, created a new consciousness of the West as
America, only more so, a region that embodies the national culture at its most energetic, rootless, complex, reactionary, subdi-
vided, wild, half-baked, comic, tragic, and hopeful. He taught
two generations of writers, and after he left teaching he continued to be both model and mentor for what has become an
explosion of literary activity in the West. And in matters of
conservation he was the most rational and eloquent of the

region's statesmen: everyone who values wilderness owes him a debt.

Did he meet the darkness with resignation and acceptance? Maybe. Certainly Wallace Stegner did not go gentle into that good night. Why should he? The moment he awoke every morning, he turned on a mind that burned like a blowtorch in the dark. Even in his advanced years he was producing brilliant work: his 1992 collection of essays, *Where the Bluebird Sings to the Lemonade Springs: Living and Writing in the West,* had been selected as a finalist for the National Book Critics Circle award, as had his previous two books, the 1987 novel *Crossing to Safety* and the 1990 *Collected Stories.* He already had a Pulitzer under his belt for the 1971 novel *Angle of Repose,* as well as a National Book Award for the 1976 novel *The Spectator Bird.* Last year the National Endowment for the Arts offered him its National Medal for the Arts, but he refused it, saying he was "troubled by the political controls placed upon the agency."

Yet neither did he rage. As always, he remained ready for the next encounter, no doubt humbled by his recent lesson in crossing to safety at night in a rented car in an unfamiliar city, but still unflinching. He spoke his last words calmly and deliberately to his doctors: "Do what you have to do."

I wish I could say that I fully understood him, for he so clearly understood himself, but though he smiled easily and often, at first the most I could grasp was that he smiled at nothing I knew.

I met Wallace Stegner on April 13, 1977. He had come to Tucson to deliver an address at the University of Arizona, where I was a graduate student in English. Within a week we had taped the first in a series of interviews and begun an exchange of letters that for sixteen years would have me checking my mailbox as expectantly as a child on the night before Christmas, long after I had embarked on a writing, teaching, and publishing career of my own.

By then he had retired from the classroom. From 1934 to 1971 he taught at universities: Utah, Wisconsin, Harvard, and finally Stanford, where he founded the creative writing program and served as its director for more than twenty-five years. At Harvard one of his students had been a pugnacious kid named Norman Mailer; at Stanford they came six at a time bearing fellowships in Stegner's name: Edward Abbey, Wendell Berry, Thomas McGuane, Larry McMurtry, N. Scott Momaday, Tillie Olsen, Robert Stone, dozens more. "The people who won fellowships in that program were so talented there would have been no holding them down," he once commented. Others who were not Stegner Fellows, including Ken Kesey, crowded into his workshops as well.

When Stewart Udall was appointed Kennedy's secretary of the interior in 1961, Stegner sent him a copy of *Beyond the Hundredth Meridian: John Wesley Powell and the Second Opening of the West*, which he had published seven years earlier. Udall's reading of the book convinced him that he needed Stegner as a special assistant; it also began something of a Democratic tradition: "I reread that book the week after I took office," Clinton's interior secretary, Bruce Babbitt, said shortly after Stegner's death— commenting also that when he first read it shortly after it was published, "It was as though someone had thrown a rock through the window."

Reduced to a message, as it often is, Stegner's 438-page "career biography" of Powell sounds hopelessly lame: development in the West will be shaped by the fact that there is enough water for only a fifth of the land. Those who actually read the book, however, like Udall and Babbitt, know that it is far richer than that. Stegner gives us what is missing from the analytic approach taken by so many historians—the living American experience, our own story—so that we can respond to it with the full power of both our intellect and our emotions.

The lack of a reasonable land policy in the West, as blatant now as it was when Stegner finished *Beyond the Hundredth Merid-*

ian forty years ago, lamentably makes the book Stegner's crown-
ing achievement in the genre. Writing it cost him some six years,
most of them spent poring through journals, dull congressional
documents, reports from the U.S. Geological Survey and the
Bureau of Ethnology, mounds of correspondence, maps, photographs, and misguided tomes, as well as Powell's own cool
tour de force, the 1878 *Report on the Lands of the Arid Region of
the United States.* Out of all that, Stegner crafted a book that not
only plunges us with Powell and his crew into the first exploration of the Colorado River, but lets us see the development of
perhaps the first grassroots environmentalist to become a savvy
dealer with government bureaucracy. We share the challenges
he faced in making himself into a naturalist and explorer with
only a homemade education; we join him in the debate with a
shortsighted, indifferent Congress bent on proliferating laws
that encourage conflict, monopoly, exploitation, and waste;
we're there as he discovers ways to influence policy and de-
construct the myth of the West as the garden of a world with
inexhaustible resources.

Powell, who died seven years before Stegner was born, did
not live to see what development would do to the dry country.
Wallace Stegner spent his life witnessing it. From his birth on
his grandfather's farm near Lake Mills, Iowa, until he "boarded
a bus in Salt Lake City to go 'back east' to graduate school in
Iowa," all the places he knew were western places: "North
Dakota wheat towns, Washington logging camps, Saskatchewan prairie hamlets and lonely homesteads, and the cities
of Seattle, Great Falls, Salt Lake, Hollywood, and Reno with
a lot of country seen on the fly between."

Wolf Willow (1962) chronicles his frontier childhood on
the family's Saskatchewan homestead. The geometric beauty
of the earth, the passion of loneliness, and the mystery of the
prairie wind blow through its pages. So do the romance and
realism of pre- and post-contact native America, the fur trade,
the Royal Canadian Mounted Police, the northward fleeing

Blackfeet, Sioux, Nez Percé, Assiniboin, and *métis,* and that booby prize of western migration, the cattle era. But the book is also haunted by the bald vulgarity of the empty American dream of something for nothing. The family that spends its summers on the homestead and its winters in town never makes its killing in wheat. Tumbleweeds take over what was once a magnificent prairie wilderness. Stegner's personal story is Powell's lesson all over again: the land will not be lived on except on its own terms.

Intimate acquaintance with the wild and wild creatures, and delayed guilt for his part in their destruction, prompted Stegner to join Bernard DeVoto's foot soldiers in the conservation wars of the forties. Much later, on a whim, he gave what he called "the labor of an afternoon" to summarizing his position on wilderness preservation—and unwittingly created a manifesto for what would become the environmental movement. Written to David E. Pesonen of the federal Outdoor Recreation Resources Review Commission in 1960—four years before Congress passed the Wilderness Act—that eight-page letter, reprinted in Stegner's 1969 essay collection *The Sound of Mountain Water,* may have done as much as anything else to save what wilderness remains in the United States. Its concluding words—"the geography of hope"—have become something of a slogan, but the letter is not an exercise in sloganeering. It stands as one of the clearest articulations of why wilderness is critical to us not only as human beings, but as Americans. "Something will have gone out of us as a people if we ever let the remaining wilderness be destroyed," Stegner wrote, "so that never again can we have the chance to see ourselves single, separate, vertical and individual in the world, part of the environment of trees and rocks and soil, brother to the other animals, part of the natural world and competent to belong in it. Without any remaining wilderness we are committed wholly, without chance for even momentary reflection and rest, to a headlong drive into our technological termite-life."

"An American," he went on, "insofar as he is new and different at all, is a civilized man who has renewed himself in the wild."

It often took a lot of persuading to move Wallace Stegner to do anything public, although privately—left to his own devices, which meant principally his writing—he helped steer the course of a civilization that continually threatened to spin out of control.

Let one instant from his boyhood serve as a parable about how he learned to deal with certain social forces. The year was probably 1918; the place, the high diving board that the editor of the town newspaper in Whitemud, Saskatchewan, had projected out over the highest cutbank of the Frenchman River (and that the editor had been the only person in town daring enough to use). It was a Sunday, and a crowd had turned out to witness the predicament of a nine-year-old boy caught in a brag. "A half-dozen times I sucked in my breath and grabbed my courage with both hands and inched out to the burlap pad on the end of the board," he would write, as an adult, decades later. "Every time, the vibrations of the board started such sympathetic vibrations in my knees that I had to creep back for fear of falling off. The crowd on the bank got scornful, and then ribald, and then insulting; I could not rouse even the courage to answer back, but went on creeping out, quaking back, creeping out again, until they finally all got tired and left for their Sunday dinners. Then at once I walked out to the end and jumped."

It would be tempting to leave him there, flailing like Icarus on the collapsed wings of his own stubborn self-reliance, had he not learned to quit despising himself for his weaknesses and ground himself in the mud of experience. But that first jump into the unknown became a leap that Wallace Stegner taught himself to make every day, quietly, unobserved, early in the morning, first up into the privacy of his own mind and then down onto the page. For months, sometimes years at a stretch, those dives at dawn submerged him in the waters of the past, where he could make connections and build the bridges to his own and his nation's identity in the present.

In 1921, three-quarters of a century after Brigham Young and the Saints, Stegner's family arrived in Salt Lake City from Canada, driving a Hudson Super Six with their "camp beds and Stoll autotent on the running boards and a big grub box on the rear bumper," fleeing failed wheat fields in his father's boomerish pursuit of instant prosperity. He was precocious, alert, intelligent, brash, challenging, literary, self-conscious, and insecure. He had already skipped a grade in school, and he soon skipped another, which meant that he weighed less than one hundred pounds his first year at East High. His weight kept him out of ROTC, which was compulsory for boys, and that rebuke stung him. Then, between his fifteenth and sixteenth years, he grew six inches. "It was like a graduation, more important to me than graduation from high school," he wrote much later, "and the beginning of the happiest years I ever knew or will know."

The next year Stegner was at the University of Utah, playing basketball and tennis, joining a fraternity and acquiring "brothers, and a secret grip, and a book of tong songs," dating girls who had towered over his head only a year earlier. One measure of his successful transfer from runt to man-on-campus appears in his grades: "straight A's as a freshman, straight B's as a sophomore."

Some of that is there in Stegner's first major novel, *The Big Rock Candy Mountain* (1943), which he finished while almost nobody was looking: snowbound in a Vermont cabin with his wife, Mary, and their son, Page, while on unpaid leave from Harvard. Virtually all of it is there in *Recapitulation,* his superb 1979 novel of the Jazz Age. The curve of his life resides in those two novels, especially in the outlines of their chief character, Bo Mason: a childhood spent in the absolute sticks; adolescence and coming of age in a provincial capital; young manhood in study and travel elsewhere to gain enlargement and perspective; and then a return to a place that enlists loyalties and demands commitment.

Sometimes the sheer stupidity of the species could goad him into action, as it did in the fifties when he joined in the race to cripple the Upper Colorado River Basin Storage Project, legislation that would have drowned much of Utah's canyon country. By 1955, thanks in part to *This Is Dinosaur: Echo Park and Its Magic Rivers,* the book of essays and photographs that the Sierra Club's David Brower convinced Stegner to edit and that Alfred Knopf rushed into print so that every member of Congress could receive a copy, two of the proposed dams were dead. Still, the legacy of that victory hung for him like a cloud over the stagnant surface of Lake Powell, formerly Glen Canyon, now choking in silt. To stop the bulldozers that developers were turning loose in the California Coast Range near his home, Stegner cofounded the Committee for Green Foothills in 1959—but like teaching and writing, his appointments to the governing boards of the Sierra Club and the Wilderness Society; to the councils of the Trust for Public Land and People for Open Space (later the Greenbelt Alliance), and to the advisory board on National Parks, Historical Sites, Buildings, and Monuments reminded him that "environmentalism or conservation or preservation, or whatever it should be called . . . is a job." He had already learned that he was not cut out to be a bureaucrat; his job with Udall lasted only a few months, after taking Udall months to persuade him to accept it.

No, what exhilarated Wallace Stegner beyond the telling were those hours spent in the twin acts of discovery and creation, writing fiction and history. Those moments, thieved from a voluntary but nevertheless indentured servitude to public life, were what he lived for.

Even as a novelist he seemed to do his best work, like that boy on the diving board, outside the public eye. For one thing, he produced much of his best work after he retired at sixty-two. The Pulitzer and the National Book Award brought him increasing national attention, but he always diverged quietly from the pursuit of fame. For another thing, Stegner challenged most of the fads and intellectual assumptions of his times—everything from Marxism to structuralism, biological determinism, magical realism, and metafiction—and whether it was a brat pack or a gathering of freeze-dried intellectuals, he never ran in a gang.

He had only friends and enemies. The enemies I know less about than the friends, but they included Ronald Reagan and James Watt and, going further back, western congressmen such as Wyoming's Frank Barrett, whose spectacular ambition it was to rescind the 1943 legislation that had created Jackson Hole National Monument and turn its elk and buffalo grounds— as well as all unreserved federal lands in the public domain—into cattle range. The friends are far too many to name. To most readers such a list would be largely meaningless anyway, although each person on it was once as essential a spoke in the wheel as the famous ones, such as Robert Frost, Frank O'Connor, Bernard DeVoto, and Ansel Adams.

To the best of the friends, Mary Page, Wallace Stegner gave everything he had from the time they were married on September 1, 1934, until his death nearly sixty years later. As one of the lesser friends, I have been lucky enough to study that marriage both up close, as it was being lived, and at a distance, through the lens of Stegner's fiction. I know enough to conclude, as others have, that insofar as they are defined by shared responsibilities and interests, loyalty, trust, pride in each other's accomplishments, earned grace and tenderness, the real and the fictional marriages are the same.

Yet the power of Stegner's fictional realism can confuse the unwary reader. The day I met him, several of my fellow students had just finished reading *Angle of Repose;* two of them, evidently expecting to see the author arrive in the wheelchair of his narrator, Lyman Ward, audibly expressed their surprise when a handsome man with a mane of white hair strode into the room propelled only by a pair of very long legs. In *Crossing to Safety*, the narrator's wife, Sally Morgan, contracts polio, and I've heard more than one reader of that novel, glimpsing Mary Stegner in the flesh, remark how relieved they were to see her walking without braces. Students of mine, writing on *All the Little Live Things*, have tried to convince me that the loss of his son in a surfing accident embittered Stegner's prose; meanwhile, Page Stegner, fifty-six, continues writing and teaching at the University of California at Santa Cruz.

Stegner's critics like to place him in the tradition of the bourgeois novel as it made its way through Balzac and Flaubert out of nineteenth-century France, into England and Russia by way of George Eliot, Trollope, Hardy, Dostoyevsky, and Tolstoy, and finally to America via Henry James, William Dean Howells, and Mark Twain. They point out that for Stegner, nature, not art, is the model, that he works from the details of ordinary settings and events to present common, ordinary lives. Even his diction and sentence structure tend toward a plain style, highlighting the story rather than the teller. Often, he leaves much of the story untold, so that the form of the novel reflects the truth that our perspectives on life are limited. Such a story ends in a given character's reflection on the failure of life to present itself in neat packages for our inspection.

By contrast, the critics point out, many of our novelists are most notable for their feats of style, writing novels that often present the unusual as if it were normal. As people, our novelists, like our poets, are more notable for their sensitivity than their balance: free to be as aberrant as their creations, whether that means manic, alcoholic, suicidal, or just plain crazy. Perhaps that's why Stegner's novels strike me as revolutionary—and why readers in the last two decades have responded to them in steadily increasing numbers. By ignoring accepted opinion and approved fashion, his novels restore a lost balance to American fiction. Stegner's characters do not challenge or defy the universe, much less despair of it. They do confront its mystery, suffer spiritual uncertainties and embarrassments, attempt reconciliations, and reconstruct values commonly forgotten, lost, or repudiated. They all move by trial and error toward dubious ends, but then that is the law of nature. Their dreams are all American dreams: not of something for nothing, but of a chance at life, safety, home, and belonging. Their questions arise from anguish and spiritual uncertainty, for they seek to impose order on their lives, to give themselves and others meaning, purpose, direction.

As for Stegner's method, anyone who wants to understand it might simply look at its equivalent in the photographs of his friend Ansel Adams: direct and undistorted, relying, in Stegner's words, not on "double exposures, the imitation of painting, the tricky lighting and artful composition," but on "found objects, natural lighting, and the clear statement of the lens." Stegner's novels, like Adams's photographs, contain the transferable currency of their creator's feelings toward his subject.

Reading back through them, I come away refreshed and invigorated, as if from a long walk outdoors. And why not? that's where they happen: mainly outside, in the last American sticks of Idaho, Utah, Montana, Wyoming, Colorado, Washington, Nevada, and California. They cross continents and borders from California to New York and Vermont, Italy, Mexico, Canada, Denmark. Whether they take me to the wilderness or a garden, a balcony in Florence or a sailboat on a Wisconsin lake, inspecting a treehouse, shooting skeet, playing tennis, or climbing in a blizzard, I come away frostbitten, bested or splashed, hungry or dirty, having not found but lost myself in places that I have come to love and so revisit again and again—almost but never quite alone, for it is in gardens that serpents reside. Still it's possible, on the long, mainly roadless ways to the homesteads, especially in Idaho or Saskatchewan, to pass sloughs aswarm with nesting geese and ducks. Sometimes we count species, the serpent and I: flickertails, prairie dogs, badgers, black-footed ferrets, coyotes, ravens, hawks. Are we home yet, Wally? How far have we come?

In all of American literature, there is nobody like Wallace Stegner, and nothing quite like his novels. He was a master of his art, and though he was a man I would have liked whether or not he had ever written a word, I will take him now wherever I can find him, and I suppose that must mean mainly in his books. I loved him. We all did. He gave us more credit than we deserved and encouraged us to undertake things we would never otherwise have dared to attempt. "All you can do is try," he would say. I can hear him now. Any minute I will look up from my desk and see him smiling.

No Agenda
but the Truth

Arthur Schlesinger, Jr.

An address delivered at the
American Academy of Arts and Letters,
November 4, 1993

THE WEST, PERCEIVED AS THE WILDERNESS, the frontier,
the virgin land, the Garden of the World, long dominated both
American history and the American imagination. If in recent
times the mystique and memory of the West have given ground
to the accelerating demands of an industrialized and urbanized
nation and an exigent and exasperating world, the West still
remains vital to our understanding of the republic—and of
ourselves as Americans. The West has undergone its share of
vicissitudes, of violations, deceptions, disillusionments, both
in actuality and in the literature. But in our own times no one
has done more to reclaim the West for American understanding,
no one has written about the meaning of the West with more
scrupulousness, perception, and wisdom, more historical objec-
tivity mingled with controlled passion, more lyrical evocation
mingled with dark foreboding, than Wallace Stegner.

Wally died last April at the age of eighty-four from injuries
received in an automobile accident. Born in Iowa in 1909, he
grew up western, as he liked to say. His family was always on
the move, pursuing an American dream that was already over
for everyone else, forever seeking that big rock candy mountain.
He never saw a water closet or a lawn, he once wrote, until he

was eleven years old. He never knew the first names of three of his grandparents. Between his twelfth and twenty-first years his family lived in twenty different houses. Neither of his parents had finished grade school.

Yet out of the chaos of his upbringing, Wally, in a recapitulation and distillation of an American experience, persevered in his own right, caught fire, worked his way through the University of Utah as a forty-hour-a-week clerk in a rug and linoleum store, took a Ph.D. at the University of Iowa, taught at the Universities of Utah and Wisconsin, then at Harvard, where I first met him in 1940, and in 1945 returned to the West he loved and found his lasting home at Stanford. He explored his West in a variety of modes—for himself, in camping on the mountains and fishing the rivers, and for the rest of us, in thirteen novels, in three volumes of short stories, in a dozen works of history and biography, and in innumerable essays.

He exulted in the West's wild beauty, in its open spaces, its dry, lucid, accurate air, its forested mountains, its geyser basins, its plateaus and mesas and canyons, its sagebrush deserts, its forms and lights and colors. He felt, as he said, "the surge of the inextinguishable western hope," the hope of building there a new civilization. But he was no sentimentalist. He saw through the myths the West contrived about itself and understood the depredations wrought by greed, by the "extractive frenzy," by the western instinct for self-destruction. He knew the damage done by those westerners who, from the white man's first invasion, pillaged the West—pillaged and ran.

Wallace Stegner belongs not only to literature but to politics in the high sense—to the formation of public policy in the interests of a civilized life. "We may love a place," he wrote, "but still be dangerous to it." His hope for the West was "a civilization to match its scenery." In the footsteps of two men about whom he wrote exemplary biographies—John Wesley Powell and Bernard DeVoto—he threw himself into the battle to preserve the West in its original contours. He was active in the Sierra Club and the Wilderness Society and in the Kennedy years served as a special assistant to Secretary of the Interior Stewart Udall. He became a vigorous participant in the fight to defend the balance of nature against "careless ruin," against the avaricious private interests, against agribusiness, against the stockmen and the miners and the grazers, and against as well the misguided public improvers, dam-builders, water-diverters, the Bureau of Reclamation and the Army Corps of Engineers; above all, against the human delusion that makes man the center of the earth and produces the "hard determination to dominate nature," the domination that drives nature in the end to exact its own revenge in grazed-over grasslands, diminished water tables, the silting and drying up of the great rivers.

But Wally never deserted the craft of literature. He was a great teacher and, as director of the Stanford Creative Writing Program, encouraged, advised, scolded, and nourished so many talented young, among them Raymond Carver, Robert Stone, Larry McMurtry, Wendell Berry, Tillie Olsen, Edward Abbey, Ernest Gaines. He cherished the hope of developing an infrastructure for literary life in the West—publishing houses, critical magazines, bookstores, a reviewing corps independent of eastern and international opinion, an alert reading public—and saw most of this come to pass.

And his own distinguished writing, in its disciplined precision, in its sense of the drama of the average, in its fidelity and grace, showed how to render the West without stereotype and melodrama. It won him the Pulitzer Prize in 1971 (for *Angle of Repose*) and the National Book Award in 1976 (for *The Spectator Bird*). In 1992, without fanfare, he declined the National Medal for the Arts in protest against the capitulation of the National Endowment for the Arts to right-wing censorship. He was always a quiet man. "In fiction," he wrote, "I think we should have no agenda but to tell the truth. The shouters in thunder roar from their podiums and pulpits. . . . They speak to the deaf, but it takes good ears to hear me, for I want to be part of the common sound, a not-too-dominating element of the ambient noise.''

His ambition was to make sense of an ordinary American life, to delineate the historic continuities between past and present and thereby to help transform natural chaos into human order. He succeeded triumphantly in his books, with their unforced penetration and power. And he succeeded triumphantly in his own life. He was not only a great teacher but a generous-hearted, warm-hearted, stout-hearted friend, a man of wry humor, imperturbable courtesy, and great charm. With Mary Stuart Page, to whom he was married for fifty-nine years, he enjoyed a personal and literary partnership of singular felicity.

Wallace Stegner reminded his nation of what it owed to the West—and reminded the West what it owed to the nation. And he did this with keen intelligence, poetic apprehension, and a serenity that will long abide.

Precedents
to Wisdom

Patricia Nelson Limerick

WALLACE STEGNER FACED FACTS, and found in those facts both
poetry and history. In a wonderful chapter in *Wolf Willow,* Stegner wrote of the town dump in Whitemud in southern Saskatchewan, where he and the other boys took up a pioneering project in
recycling. When they brought items they discovered at the dump
back to the town, adult reaction was not overwhelmingly enthusiastic. "Occasionally," Stegner wrote, "something we really valued with a passion was snatched from us in horror and returned
at once. That happened to the mounted head of a white mountain goat, somebody's trophy from old times and the far Rocky
Mountains, that I brought home one day. My mother took one
look and discovered that his beard was full of moths." "I remember that goat," Stegner ended this passage from *Wolf Willow;* "I
regret him yet. Poetry is seldom useful, but always memorable."

Stegner knew that the workings of human memory and loyalty
are as funny as they are powerful. In Sacramento last February,
responding to a panel presentation of writers discussing his
work, Mr. Stegner said, "I want to protest first, to all of you.
Not one of you, in all this laudatory talk, has mentioned my
sense of humor."

Wallace Stegner was a man of humor, and of great foresight,
and of wisdom. If you spend your days in a university, "wisdom"
is not a word that you hear much. You hear a lot about research
and scholarship, but the word wisdom never comes up when vice

chancellors and deans gather to discuss the agenda of the university. This is one of the main reasons why the public does not feel much affection for universities, and why the public thinks that scholarly writing is a self-indulgent habit of professors, without much value to anyone outside the university. The troubled state of affairs in higher education adds up to one major reason why Wallace Stegner's example is so compelling and urgent today. He was not a man in flight from the word wisdom.

In 1945, Wallace Stegner, in collaboration with the editors of *Look* magazine, published a book called *One Nation*. When you look at this book, one set way of thinking about Wallace Stegner's work collapses. "Stegner," this pattern of thought runs, "was great on environmentalism, and very much ahead of his time in paying attention to women as morally complex, significant characters in fiction, but ethnic issues were not really his concern." I was myself long under the impression that if you were in the market for precedents in wisdom in environmental affairs, you went to Stegner, and if you wanted precedents in wisdom in race relations, you went to Carey McWilliams.

Look at *One Nation*, and you learn that Stegner was just as dramatically ahead of his time in the matter of race relations as he was in environmental affairs. "There is a wall down the middle of America," Stegner said in the opening pages of *One Nation*, "a wall of suspicion, distrust, snobbery, hatred, and guilt. On one side is the majority of our people—white, Protestant, and gentile. . . . On the other side are people who because of color, religion, or cultural background are not allowed to be full citizens of the United States."

It would not take a particularly acute thinker to make this observation in 1993, or in 1963, for that matter. But a white writer *in 1945*, attacking the injustice of segregation and discrimination and launching that attack in a very public arena, adds up to a remarkable and inspirational sight to contemplate. Stegner himself referred to *One Nation* as a "wartime-patriotism" book. This reference might be puzzling, until you realize that Stegner meant *true* patriotism—not an unthinking round of applause for a great country, but an appraisal of the nation's real situation, an appraisal with a critical and ethical edge. Patterns of racial injustice that "we have permitted," Stegner wrote, "have a clear relationship with Nazi practices; the difference is only a difference in degree. . . . The Nazi cult of 'race' purity . . . has its exponents in America, and always has had." He gave no white Americans a comfortable exemption: "None of us is so different from the classic Southerner, the unreconstructed Johnny Reb. The germs of prejudice are as common as those of tuberculosis: most of us under the x-ray would show the [signs] of old infections."

Stegner did not give an inch to any wartime impulse to offer an upbeat or sanitized version of American history. "Two of our minority groups," he said, "are conquered peoples—the Indians and the Spanish colonists of the Southwest," while blacks came in a "forced immigration," and even immigrants who came by choice entered a nation that "showed ugly signs of class and caste distinctions and an ugly will to resent or suspect the foreign and the strange." In the years since the conquest, Indians, Stegner said, had "suffered almost as much from our indifference and our charity as they did earlier from our Manifest Destiny." "Prejudice against the first Americans still persists," he wrote, "and there are still plenty of people quite willing to go back to the exploitation and robbery that we practiced for two hundred and fifty years."

Stegner was just as clearsighted in his discussion of the history of Mexicans and Mexican-Americans. For Mexican workers employed by "large-scale farm operators," he said, "working for such operators has been a kind of slavery." And, anticipating what is currently a huge issue in the West, Stegner captured the difficulties raised by shifting an economy toward tourism and offering a romanticized, colorful history for sale. Many Mexican-Americans and Mexican immigrants, he wrote, "neither can be nor want to be 'professional Mexicans' for the amusement of tourists in such 'quaint' sections as Los Angeles' Olvera Street.

With some justice they commonly feel that everything Mexican in California is picturesque except the Mexican people."

When one reaches Stegner's discussion of police brutality toward minorities, the urge—to look back at the publication date and make sure that it *really* says 1945—becomes overpowering. Almost fifty years before the name Rodney King became famous, he wrote that "police protection is too frequently something to make a Negro or Mexican shut his teeth together and bite off the things he wants to say. It is no secret that many police departments have their quota of sadists who operate by preference on the helpless—and no other grown man in America is likely to be quite so helpless as a member of a disliked and branded minority." On the chance that some of his readers might take him to mean that a few bad policemen were corrupting a basically sound system, Stegner pulled out the stops: "The law and order which the police are sworn to protect is the law and order of the ruling caste and class and color and faith, and so one is not surprised when Los Angeles police, faced with the problem of a dead Mexican in the street, put out a dragnet and sweep in three hundred Mexican youths on suspicion. . . . As long as we hire police we should expect them to do our collective will. The reason behind the frequent indifference of the police to the rights of minorities is the collective will of the society which hires them."

There is not an enormous amount of text in *One Nation*, because it is also full of pictures. But, short or not, it is a remarkable text for the tranquility, measured pace, and thoroughness of its coverage. Stegner does not, for instance, waste any time on lamentations over the usual, East Coast–centered picture of American race relations. He does not bother to denounce the limits of that model; he simply puts forward a better and more accurate one. The book begins in the West and, quietly reversing the usual, set, unthinking, east-to-west directionality of American history, begins with Filipinos, Japanese-Americans, Chinese-Americans, Mexicans, Hispanos, and Indians, and then turns to eastern locations for three groups, blacks, Catholics, and Jews. The text is centered in the West for seven of its group portraits, with only the last five portraits drawn from the eastern United States.

From the first page, Stegner made it clear that he was not going to fall back on the usual pattern of thought that comes as a direct result of failure to take the West seriously. He would not take the idea of "American race relations" to mean a bipolar relationship between blacks and whites. On this matter and many others, Stegner was far ahead of his time in 1945. He is, in fact, still ahead of *our* time, in 1993.

Stegner found space in his brief text for another important, and too often evaded issue. Prejudices and stereotypes, he said, "can even infect minority groups themselves—set one group off against another, breed a narrow group spirit that can be fatal to any hope of ultimate harmony." There are Jews who are anti-Semites, Stegner noted; while a "snobbish dislike for lower-class Negroes is by no means uncommon among Negroes who have climbed above the average level." The dangers of stereotyping appeared in every relationship. "It is as dangerous," Stegner said in a line well worth pondering, "for a Negro to think of the generalized 'white man' as it is for a white man to create and then abuse an abstract 'Negro.' "

Stegner had clearly and accurately sized up the meaning of his historical moment: "Whether we like it or not, World War Two has been a war of liberation. It will not be possible in any foreseeable future to run a white man's world with yellow or black or brown colonies whose exploitation supports it." The United States was not quarantined from the broad patterns of change on the planet. "It becomes increasingly clear," Stegner concluded, "that racial and religious tensions are the gravest threat to the future that we face."

There are some clear "signs of the times" in *One Nation*, of course, references to "simple" and "primitive" cultures, for instance, references that do not sound anywhere nearly as hip as the passages I have quoted. But even with a few of the more

dated elements included, what Stegner said in the 1940s is still
what we need to hear, and to act on, in the 1990s. My point, moreover, is *not* that Stegner was "politically correct" long before the
term was invented. My point is that Stegner was factually correct and ethically correct, and we are much in his debt because
he said these things so clearly and so forcefully, before many others were saying them, or even thinking them. He warned Americans in 1945 that they ran the risk of "Balkanizing the nation,
splitting it into mutually repellent fragments." The warning
stands, having only gained in relevance.

One Nation, with its full ethnic inclusiveness and demand
for justice, with its careful attention to the significance of the
western half of the United States in the picture of national race
relations, was evidence enough that Stegner had the jump on
the New Western History. Both the method and the content of
his story in *Wolf Willow* proved the case again. This was place-
centered history, beginning with the physical environment,
tracking the presence of Indians, telling the full story of the
complicated events and maneuverings—of Indians, *métis*, Hudson's Bay Company traders, and Mounties—that had preceded
the arrival of white American farmers. This was a history that
faced up to tragedy and failure, and to brutality as well, and connected the whole package of the past up to the environmental
and human issues of the present.

As a child in Whitemud, Stegner learned nothing about the
history of the place where he lived. The chimneys of an abandoned *métis* village stood near his town, and no one knew what
they were; "we never so much as heard the word *métis*," he
wrote. Instructed in the history of the distant places, he lived
in the Cypress Hills without "the faintest notion of who had
lived there before me." The Cypress Hills and Whitemud offered all the elements of "a past to which I could be tribally
and emotionally committed," he wrote; his home had all
"the associations with which human tradition defines and en-
riches itself"—but no one knew, and no one told the children.

Repeatedly, Stegner declared in *Wolf Willow* that he wished he had been told this history as a child, given some moorings in his particular place, allowed to know that significant human events had happened in his home, and not just in places far to the east. These declarations go right to the core of the new western history. His desire for "a past to which [he] could be tribally and emotionally committed" expresses exactly what I, and many others, wanted but could not get from the old western history.

In his writing of place-centered history, Stegner had again jumped ahead of his time. In fact, most western writers—historians as well as novelists—were at the very same time resolutely jumping *behind* their times, jumping backward into a remote and unconnected frontier past. In an essay published in 1967, "History, Myth, and the Western Writer," Stegner used the important and memorable phrase "the amputated Present," to describe this failure to connect. "Western writers," Stegner said, "have shown a disinclination, perhaps an emotional inability to write about the contemporary." Through all "the newly swarming regions of the West," he wrote, "millions of westerners, old and new, have no sense of a personal and *possessed* past, no sense of any continuity between the real western past which has been mythicized almost out of recognizability and a real western present that seems as cut-off and pointless as a ride on a merry-go-round that can't be stopped."

Twenty-six years ago, Wallace Stegner challenged western historians to stop amputating the present from the past. Fifty years ago, he wrote a text that put the great ethnic diversity of the West permanently on record. And yet professional western historians neither responded to his challenge nor imitated his example. Stegner had the strange and ironic experience of writing in several genres and crossing between the disciplines just at the historical moment when the boundaries between the disciplines were hardening and rigidifying. But things have changed. This is, in fact, one of the most interesting, distinctive, and exciting things happening now in western intellectual affairs: everybody is reading everybody else—academics reading nonacademics, writers of fiction reading writers of nonfiction, and people with doctorates in history taking Wallace Stegner seriously as a thinker about the field.

Back in Whitemud, Saskatchewan, Stegner had only one place to go to learn about local history, and that place was the dump, the place "that contained relics of every individual who had ever lived" in town. In the artifacts of that dump, and in the unbridled enthusiasm that Stegner and his friends had for examining those artifacts, we get a very close analogy to the spirit of the new western history. As the boys of Whitemud knew, it does not make any sense to go to the dump in order to *edit* it, to look only for positive and inspirational relics. You examine everything, whether it is attractive or not, because you want to understand the *whole* past, not a selected and prettified version of it. Indeed, those who have complained of the harsh realism and "negativity" of the new western history might thank their lucky stars that they were spared participation in the exploration of the Whitemud Dump. In one memorable passage, Stegner described a "welter of foul-smelling feathers and coyote-scattered carrion, that was all that remained of somebody's dream of a chicken ranch. The chickens had all got some mysterious pip at the same time, and died as one, and the dream lay out there with the rest of the town's short history. . . ." To Stegner the town dump, in all its mixed contents, "was our poetry and our history." That statement goes a long way to explaining why western creative writers and western historians have found a shared cause in their exploration of the western past, with Wallace Stegner as the guide we have in common.

Remembering
Wallace Stegner

James D. Houston

HE WAS THE STEADIEST MAN I have ever known, steady in his habits, steady in his tastes, in his view of the world. I met him in 1961, last saw him in February 1993, and in all those years the essential things about him had not changed. He knew his mind. He answered his mail. He got his work done in a way that generated the unflagging admiration of any writer who knew the depth of his commitment to the task itself, the daily task. In his eyes there was always a look that matched the effect of his stories—probing, unswerving, humane. Like so many of his characters, Wally Stegner looked straight at the physical and social world and did not flinch at what he saw.

He had a ground-wire that ran deep and kept him anchored to the earth and to the earthly places that had been important to him. In his day-to-day living, and in all of Stegner's books, the sense of place has been essential to an understanding of the life. One such place was East End, Saskatchewan, where he spent several boyhood years, a town he often circled back to—in *On a Darkling Plain* (1940), and in his first big success, *The Big Rock Candy Mountain* (1943), and in *Wolf Willow* (1962). Another is Salt Lake City, where he grew up and went to college, locale for his 1979 novel, *Recapitulation,* wherein a man returns to his hometown, plays the past against the present, and brings his life full circle. Coast Range mountainsides, like those surrounding his Los Altos Hills home of forty-five years, provided backdrops for the 1967 novel, *All the Little Live Things,* as well as for major portions of his Pulitzer Prize–winning masterpiece, *Angle of Repose* (1971).

Stegner's sense of place and sense for the West as a region involved a good deal more than setting, a good deal more than the skill to evoke a landscape or the feel of a town, what they used to call "local color." Something elemental about the West emerges, comes pushing through his prose. You feel it in numerous individual works, but more impressively in the body of his work taken as a whole, the novels and short stories, the histories and biographies, together with his labors as an active conservationist—the wide-ranging output of his long and amazingly productive career.

Built into these works are levels of perception that come at you sometimes all at once, sometimes singly, like strata seen in a canyon wall. There is the physical and geological West, as an awesome stretch of the Earth's landscape. There is the legendary West, as a vast repository for illusion and fantasy and improbable hope. There is the cultural West, forever locked in its love-hate embrace with the cultural East. And there is the historical West, with its violent and rapacious past that must be understood if we are to survive the present, not to mention the future.

In Stegner's world you do not find many shootouts or Apache raiders looming at the mountain rim to swoop down on a hapless wagon train. "The western past," he said in 1974, "in a lot of people's minds, is the mythic past of the horse opera, which is no past at all. It is an illusion."

Among his few cowboys is Ray Wiley, in the vintage story "Carrion Spring" (from *Wolf Willow*). Ray's adversary is not a band of outlaws. It is the weather. In the brutal Saskatchewan winter of 1907 he watches thousands of cattle freeze to death. At the taut conclusion, while carcasses rot in the spring thaw, the cowboy decides to stay on, to gut it out, in spite of this disaster. Why? He can't exactly say. There is a challenge of such magnitude, he can't bear not to try again. There is also something about the land, the

very look of the land. Just as winter turns to spring, the spark
of hope flares one more time.

A more characteristic hero in Stegner country is John Wesley
Powell, the real-life subject of his novelized biography, *Beyond
the Hundredth Meridian*. Powell was a naturalist, an explorer,
a nineteenth-century visionary whose showdown came not
in the streets of Dodge City but in the halls of Congress, where
his plan for a manageable water policy for the western states
was shot down by the heavy guns of expansionism and run-
away development.

Published in 1954, this is essential reading for anyone who
wants to understand the role of water in the evolution of western
America. The sixty pages describing Powell's harrowing boat trip
down the Colorado and through the Grand Canyon are in themselves worth the price of admission. And the issues Powell raised
in the 1870s and 1880s, raised again by Stegner in the 1950s, are
still with us, supporting his contention, as both historian and
novelist, that the past illuminates the present—a family's past,
a river's past, a region's past—as surely as a coastline or a prairie
or a mountain range can bear upon one's character, one's
dreams, one's worldview.

I feel compelled to mention one more book, less known and
seldom talked about these days, because it has been out of print
for a number of years. But it had a good long life, after it was
published in the final year of World War Two, and it represents
another defining feature of Stegner's vision. He titled it *One Nation*. As time goes by, this book becomes, in my opinion, ever
more significant. It's a pioneering study of the United States as
a mosaic of many co-existing peoples. These sentences come
from the Introduction:

*No other nation on earth has had the opportunity the United States has
had to bring so many peoples and cultures together into one society, to learn
from all of them, to grow by the contributions that all have made. It follows
that no other nation, despite the tragic failures of our principles in many
instances, has come so close to promoting a real brotherhood of man. With-*

out our minority groups and the diverse strains of our culture, American society is a pale imitation of Europe. With them, it is something newer and stronger.

But it follows just as surely that our failure—if we fail—to make a place for everybody in that society will be a blow disastrous to the hope for peace in the world. For if we cannot do it, within the boundaries of one continental nation, under one democratic government, with a tradition of political ideals as high as any nation ever aspired to, how can it be done in the world of nations whose sole tradition has been suspicion, spheres of influence, and balances of power, and whose blood burns with hatreds generations old?

The problem of the populations of America, the problem of making one nation from the many races and creeds and kinds, one culture from all the European, Indian, African and Asiatic cultures that the promise of freedom has drawn to our shores, comes to a head in our time. Its solution is the absolutely essential first step of a process which is historically inevitable, but which can be materially hastened by the efforts of any American with the imagination and the good will to work at it.

This sounds like something that could have been written fairly recently, perhaps within the past couple of years. Such ideas are very much in the air these days. But Stegner did not write this book last month. Or last year. *One Nation* came out in 1945, when very few people dared to talk this kind of talk. In 1945 my wife, Jeanne, was still in an internment camp called Manzanar over in the Owens Valley, in the high desert beyond the Sierra Nevada range, along with ten thousand other Americans of Japanese background. That was the climate in 1945, and Stegner's was one of the few voices speaking out with fervor that there was another way to look at individuals and to think about their histories and their humanity. It is just one more example of what he has done for us all, over the years, as a writer, as a historian and storyteller, as a man of the western United States.

Last February many of these concerns were still on Stegner's mind. In Sacramento, the Center for California Studies was holding its annual conference on the state of the state. "Reassembling

California" was this year's theme, and the three-day event was dedicated to Wally, as a writer and a teacher whose work had touched just about every aspect of our western life. Knowing he would be on hand, a large crowd turned out for a Friday morning panel called "The Range of Vision: Wallace Stegner and the West." Four of us had been invited to speak: Patricia Limerick, the University of Colorado historian; Al Young from Palo Alto, a former Stegner Fellow; Gerald Haslam, writer and editor from Sonoma State; and me. At the end of the session Wally took the stage and talked for about ten minutes. This was one of his last public appearances, and for most of us there it was the last time we would see him.

We had talked about his fiction, his historical work, about his time in Washington, D.C., when Stewart Udall was Secretary of the Interior, and about the writing program he established at Stanford. Several questions from the audience had touched upon the role of regions and places, and he came back to this, our attitudes toward the places we inhabit, invoking Mary Austin and finally invoking John Wesley Powell.

"He was right more than a hundred years ago when he said that in the West there is water enough for about a fifth of the land. And that means no matter what you do with it, whether you're going to manufacture with it, whether you're going to have cities, going to use it for agriculture—there is water for about a fifth of the land. And thank God that will leave us some open space, I think, for quite some time."

His voice, as he said these things, was a voice I had been hearing for over thirty years, on and off the page, a voice that requires you to listen, a voice both deliberate and spirited. There was something of the minister in Wally Stegner, though not the haranguing kind; he was a scrupulously moral writer but not a moralizer. There was something of the prophet about him too, but not the Jeremiah kind. His grasp of history gave him a window on the future, but he leavened his warnings with compassion and a careful, hard-earned wisdom.

As he spoke that morning I remember thinking that he looked remarkably fit for eighty-four. He had vigor. His eyes were bright. His newest book was in the stores—*Where the Bluebird Sings to the Lemonade Springs*—and he had readings lined up. At the time there was every reason to believe he would be with us for a good while longer. It made his untimely death in Santa Fe last month a double shock. He passed away too suddenly, and too soon. But his works live on, and they will be with us for a long time to come, a lifetime of solid prose. In six decades of writing he gave us twenty-eight books, plus countless essays, articles, and stories, along with a way of looking at America and at the American West, and a way of seeing more and knowing more about ourselves.

Where the
Bluebird Sings

Gretchen Holstein Schoff

Now we are finally here. This, in all its painful ambiguity, is
what we came for.

CROSSING TO SAFETY

IT HAPPENED, on a brilliant May morning in 1986, that Patricia
Anderson, Professor Walter Ridcout, and I stood at the front
door of a home in the village of Shorewood Hills, and Wallace
Stegner answered the bell.

More than nostalgia must have been on Stegner's mind that
spring morning. He had come back to Madison to receive an hon-
orary degree from the University of Wisconsin. The university
was the place where Stegner had spent some of his first lean
years as an academic—teaching, correcting student papers, and
working "around the edges" and far into the night on launching
his own writing career. Madison had been the seedbed for friendships and emotional relationships that lasted all his life, and by
the time Stegner returned, he had honed "returning" to an art.
Writing *Wolf Willow* and *The Sound of Mountain Water* had taught
him how much could be learned by going back, checking memory against reality.

And in 1986 he had another project in the works. His novel

Crossing to Safety was published in 1987. Much of the story has Madison as its setting, though, clearly, emotional landscapes, more than lakes and hills, count most in this book. As Stegner was to put it later: "Of all the books I ever wrote, *Crossing to Safety* is in some ways the most personal. It is, in fact, deliberately close to my own experiences, opinions, and feelings, which are refracted through a narrator not too different from myself."

Crossing to Safety tells the story of an important relationship between two academic couples, one wealthy, the other struggling to get a start (as Stegner and his wife were in the 1930s). Stegner called the themes of the novel "love, friendship, and survival" and the villains of the novel "willfulness, polio, cancer, and blind chance."

So to say that *Crossing to Safety* was on his mind in 1986 is too mild a statement. Stegner, somewhat later, put it this way: "I wrote my guts out trying to make it as moving on the page as it was to me while I was living and reliving it."

> *You don't go out and "commit experience" for the sake of writing about it later; and if you have to make notes on how a thing has struck you, it probably hasn't struck you.*
> ON THE TEACHING OF CREATIVE WRITING

Inevitably, Stegner admirers in Madison looked for ways to make good use of his time during that commencement weekend, one of the ways being to request an interview for broadcast over the state radio network. Stegner agreed, but asked that the interview be conducted, not at the station, but at the home of friends with whom he was staying. Patricia Anderson, then executive director of the Wisconsin Humanities Committee, arranged for the interview. (At her encouragement, the committee had commissioned Stegner to write a special essay, "Sense of Place," which had been published in a limited edition under committee auspices by Silver Buckle Press at the University of Wisconsin–Madison. Stegner regarded this essay as important enough to be included in his last published collection, *Where the Bluebird Sings to the Lemonade Springs*.)

I was afraid of that first encounter. I have had more disappointments than I care to mention meeting "famous writers," watching them diminish, shrivel, indulge in displays of ego or eccentricity. I was not overawed at the prospect of meeting Stegner. I was afraid he would have feet of clay, that I would be disappointed to meet in the flesh the image and voice I had come to love on the page.

The door opened and the "sizing up" came first—so much is conveyed in the first minute. If he felt reluctant or thought of the morning ahead as a nettling obligation, he gave no sign. He smiled and welcomed us. Casually dressed in a figured knit sweater, tan trousers, comfortable shoes, he moved across the room and sat down with the grace of a man much younger than his years. He had a sense of style, a presence—snow-white hair, a quiet dignified bearing. Most arresting of all were his easy laugh and his eyes. He was a born listener and told you, with his gaze, that what you were saying had his attention. Whatever fear of disappointment I brought along dropped away at the doorsill.

Other details struck me. Stegner was missing a finger on one hand (below the second knuckle) and I wondered how it had happened; it made me think of farm boys I'd known who lost fingers in corn choppers or on power take-offs. The longer I watched Stegner the more familiar he seemed, like the Scandinavian men I had known all my life—my father, grandfather, uncles, cousins, my husband. There was that fundamental strength and muscle of the body, the strength acquired through hard work in youth, strength that never completely fades. There was the wry humor. Most of all, there was Nordic understatement. (Is it the Scandinavian "iceberg syndrome"—nine-tenths of the significance concealed below the surface?) Stegner was, by 1986, winner of a Pulitzer Prize, a National Book Award, dozens of other awards and prizes—a giant of a writer who had shown that he could do it all: novels, short stories, essays, history, biography, reportage. But he talked about his writing craft that morning with the modesty of the Wimbledon champ who says he plays a little tennis.

> . . . *a novel is a long, long agony. When Bill Styron described it as like setting out to walk from Vladivostok to Spain on your knees, he was not just making a phrase.*
> ON THE TEACHING OF CREATIVE WRITING

We talked of many things that morning, about writers like Beryl Markham and Isak Dinesen, about the triangulations and plotting in *Angle of Repose*, about teaching writing and about doing your historical homework.

At one point I asked, "How long did it take you to write *Beyond the Hundredth Meridian?*"

"Eleven years," he answered. *Beyond the Hundredth Meridian*, the biography of John Wesley Powell, sets one of the great benchmarks for writing about the West. It is a masterwork of dazzling virtuosity, weaving together history, geography, biography, geology—a tale of rivers and mountains and short grass prairie, of whites and Indians.

"How did you know what questions to ask yourself, or where to look for answers?" I asked.

Stegner stopped, smiling slightly at the memory of what the book must have taken out of him.

"Sometimes I didn't know. Whenever I needed to know what to do next, I'd ask Benny. Benny knew everything about the West. Benny was loaded." (One of Stegner's most loving pieces is his memoir of Bernard DeVoto, *The Uneasy Chair*.)

I took no notes that day, but the morning with Wallace Stegner struck me. It has stayed with me ever since. What can you see in two or three hours? Certainly not the warts, the sins of omission and commission. (Who among us is without them, but they were territory reserved for the people who knew him well, lived with him, worked with him.) I wasn't canonizing him for sainthood, but I walked down the drive of that house in Shorewood Hills thinking, "What you see on the page is what you get in the flesh."

The work and the man seemed as close to seamless as one could hope for, expressions of one another, a rarity in any life.

> *Largeness is a lifelong matter. . . . You grow because you*
> *are not content* not *to. You are like a beaver that chews*
> *constantly because if it doesn't, its teeth grow long and lock.*
> *You grow because you are a grower; you're large because you*
> *can't stand to be small.*
>
> ON THE TEACHING OF CREATIVE WRITING

The phone rang half a dozen times before 10:00 A.M. Three of the callers eased into it with, "Have you seen the morning paper?" Two simply blurted it out. "Stegner died yesterday." The sixth was already thinking ahead. "We should do something, some kind of memorial meeting, talking about his work, something. I'm not quite sure what."

All over America, ink will flow, now that Stegner has died. So many different kinds of people staked out claims on him— friends and family, environmentalists, historians, westerners, his writing students, colleagues. He had covered a lot of ground.

The environmentalists owe him. He didn't whine or sermonize; he just turned a formidable talent to things he believed in. People like Stegner and DeVoto had a parade started on wilderness long before there was a bandwagon, before Earth Day had become a catchword. Stegner's essay on Dinosaur National Monument, though written in the 1950s, could have been written yesterday. He was already worried about the day when human beings might have only one square foot of ground to themselves, and no place to run to. He also understood the West, how inextricably its history, its myths and delusions, its angst are tied to the presence or absence of water. Aridity has always driven the destiny of the West, and few writers knew the particulars better than Stegner. What he learned writing *Beyond the Hundredth Meridian*, he came back to again and again—in *The West as Living Space, The Sound of Mountain Water,* and *Wolf Willow.*

So a host of westerners, writers like Ivan Doig, Larry McMurtry, Edward Hoagland, will remember what Stegner taught them about themselves. If there really is such a thing as an ethos of a region, Stegner went very far in shaking out the ingredients—individualism, loneliness, ego, rapacity. Missing from the crew who remember, and it's a pity, will be Edward Abbey, whose outrageousness was full of surprises; Abbey always could be counted on to skip being too reverent or solemn. He was amused at the way regionalism was turning into a writing industry, and he once remarked that regional writers were crawling all over the landscape, staking out territories "like vacuum cleaner salesmen." Stegner managed to be larger than that—interpreting the West, but slipping past the regional label.

Historians owe Stegner too. He showed that he could do his homework on the facts, corroborating where he was able and admitting he couldn't when he was unable. Further, he demonstrated in *Wolf Willow* how he thought history was a pontoon bridge and its building materials a mixture of verifiable fact, memory, and autobiography. The histories we get, Stegner believed, depend on which stories historians choose to tell, what questions they ask, and ultimately on the artistry they summon to set the stories down. Whether historians agree or not with the Stegner idea of historiography, they can't have failed to notice what powerful storytelling history can be or what a writer can do with a prose style that has no fat. Readers can learn as much about how America was transformed, grabbed, explored, and exploited from Stegner's short essay "Inheritance" as they can from a shelf full of ponderous historical treatises.

Then there are Stegner's students, the writers he helped all those years. Hundreds of writers got their start at Stanford when Stegner led the Creative Writing Program there. Festschrifts are probably bubbling all over the place, because long after writers left the school, they kept sending Stegner galleys. By all accounts, the Stegner touch was a blend of expectation and respect. His expectations were rigorous—he was a bear about grammar, impatient with phoniness or missed deadlines. No excuses. You put your seat on the seat of the chair, and you write. And it had better be seven days a week, "not six, not five—certainly not two or three."

As for the respect, he seemed to have little taste for personality cults or for creating clones of himself. Take a look at his alumni list if you need proof. A writing school that has nurtured the likes of Wendell Berry, Tillie Olsen, Ken Kesey, must have been a place that knew how to spot "promise" on the application form and, once writers got there, didn't encourage cliques or clones.

Every writer knows how lonely a business it is, how dull facing the wall can be. Brotherhoods develop among those who face the wall. Stegner sometimes wrote to the brotherhood, pieces like his wonderful "Letter to Wendell Berry" and his moving response, probably the best yet written, to Maclean's *A River Runs through It*. It's a pity, too, that Maclean, like Abbey, is not around to say goodbye. He would have known what Stegner was trying to do. Both men had grown beyond their westernness, without ever losing a sense of how it shaped them. Both lived long lives, years that spanned an incredible century. Both lived long enough to fish the river of time. Both knew what it meant to lay the line down in a perfect cast with their words, and then to enjoy the quiet pleasure, as Maclean put it, of "watching yourself softly becoming the author of something beautiful."

In a lot of ways, it's the people who won't write tributes, don't know how to say goodbye, who will miss Stegner the most. With all the public acclaim that gathered momentum in the last years of his life, it is doubtful that he realized how many garden-variety readers he had, people who love books and regard them much as they do favorite friends. Stegner never caved in to fads, never reached for the bizarre, the decadent, the arty. That was his great art, the control of a sentence that lesser writers would kill for and the genius to take dailiness and turn it into transcendence.

Readers recognized the sound of an American voice. They

waited for it and took comfort that it was there, as children do who hear the murmur of grown-up voices in distant rooms. When they read, "I may not know who I am, but I know where I am from," they got the message. Stegner wasn't so much telling them who he was; he was telling them how to find out who they were.

> *There is no decent literature on how to die. There ought to be, but there isn't. . . . Medical literature is all statistics. So I'm having to find my own way.*
>
> CROSSING TO SAFETY

This remembrance, much too late, recalls a brief encounter with Wallace Stegner. The blink of an eye, for him, but I wanted him to know the encounter "stuck." I caught him, that day, shuttling back and forth between inner and outer landscapes. In 1986 he was seventy-seven years old, and still growing. Three years later, at eighty, he sat down and wrote a long overdue letter to his mother:

Mom, listen. [That's the way he starts.] *Except when I have to tie my shoe-laces, I don't feel eighty years old. . . . But if I don't feel decrepit, neither do I feel wise or confident. Age and experience have not made me a Nestor qualified to tell others how to live their lives. . . . Instead of being embittered, or stoical or calm, or resigned, or any of the standard things that a long life might have made me, I confess that I am often simply lost, as much in need of comfort, understanding, forgiveness, uncritical love—the things you used to give me—as I ever was at five, or ten, or fifteen.* (Where the Bluebird Sings to the Lemonade Springs)

What an admission! So there is no decent literature on how to die? Well, then, you do the next best thing. What Wallace Stegner left behind was the road map from the Big Rock Candy Mountain to the land where the bluebird sings. This is what he came for, to tell the long, broken story of crossing to safety, with all its painful ambiguity.

A Tribute to
Wallace Stegner

David E. Bonior

THIS IS AN UNUSUAL CIRCUMSTANCE for me. I am obviously out of place as a literary critic. The language of good writing rarely finds its way into politics. Carefully crafted images in a fine story have little in common with the rough and tumble of debate. Lyrical descriptive passages are far from the hackneyed stuff of press releases or the technical jargon of legislation.

So I cannot speak here in the voice of an expert. I come in appreciation of Wallace Stegner. And, no matter how haltingly and inadequately, to say thank you to him as well.

Surprisingly, Stegner entered my life in a political setting. And perhaps he has held me spellbound in part because of my life in politics. When Carla Cohen invited me to participate in this special evening, she suggested I might speak to the unique appeal Wallace Stegner has in Washington. So I began remembering.

I was in a small office in the Capitol then—just myself and

three staff. We were working to try to bring peace to Central America. Wonderful people visited us. People who also cared deeply about justice in those small, distant countries. One of those friends was David Cohen.

At the end of a particularly long and arduous day, we collapsed in the office—David, my three staff—Kathy, Jerry, and Judy—and myself. We talked of what we were reading. David mentioned a new novel by a favorite author—*Crossing to Safety*, by Wallace Stegner.

Embarrassingly, none of us knew of the author or the book! I went first, but we all fell in love. We were elated that we had so much catching up to do. Soon we were exchanging earlier works as gifts, borrowing from libraries, searching through used book stores, visiting Politics and Prose. The four of us have shared Wallace Stegner in the office almost as if he were one of us.

And many of you too felt that same sense of connection. You knew he would be a lovely man. We fantasized about inviting him to visit our office to sit and talk with us. We all made pilgrimages to hear him read.

Why? Why did we feel so passionately about this writer? We've heard Mr. Watkins talk about the man—his dignity, his conviction, his forthrightness. We've heard Alan Cheuse read his prose—the clarity, the sense of time and place, the values.

Everything he was and represents is where we each came from and why we are here.

Political Washington is truly a mad, mad world. If you do not know who you are when you get here, you will be lost forever. Not only must you know, but you must remember. And Wallace Stegner reminds us to think about where we came from—our own personal sense of place and a reverence for that land. He prods us to re-examine the basic values of trust and friendship and respect.

From that tiny, windowless office, Wallace Stegner opened the back doors of our lives.

We were lured west by the promise of an awakening America in *Angle of Repose*. We were sucked into the endless, beckoning, threatening horizon in *The Big Rock Candy Mountain*. We squeezed the dirt between our toes again in *Wolf Willow*. We tottered on the balance beam between generations in *All the Little Live Things*. We revered friendship anew in *Crossing to Safety*.

That which many of us have lost by coming here we regained through Wallace Stegner. We came from a beautiful land to be always indoors. We came because we cared in some fundamental way about helping people to a city where even friendship is a chameleon.

Is it any wonder that in Washington our very souls would be touched by a writer who muses:

Friendship is a relationship that has no formal shape, there are no rules or obligations or bonds as in marriage or the family. It is held together by neither law nor property nor blood, there is no glue in it but mutual liking. It is therefore rare.

We know how rare it is—especially here. We treasure anyone who can illuminate our own internal guideposts to help us, may I say, cross safely.

We four are still together and here tonight—Kathy Gille, Jerry Hartz, and now my wife, Judy. We are in a far larger office now—many rooms, even windows. Life is more hectic than ever. But we mourned Wallace Stegner's death the way we celebrated his life—by sharing.

Stegner's work connects me with myself. His writing refreshes and invigorates me. He compels me to be steadfast, to remember who I am. He holds so firmly to the real truths, the real values.

Life is hard. But when it hurts he is also here with that simple last line from *All the Little Live Things:*

I shall be richer all my life for this sorrow.

And aren't we all richer for Wallace Stegner.

Partnership with the Land

Bruce Babbitt

Remarks in remembrance of Wallace Stegner,
delivered at the Interior South Building,
Washington, D.C., April 22, 1993

I'D LIKE TO JUST SHARE WITH YOU my first encounter with
Wallace Stegner. It was, as I suppose with most of us, an encounter with a book. I grew up in a small resource town on
the Colorado plateau, imprisoned by the mythology of an in-
dividualistic West, and surrounded by the stories of individuals who had conquered the West. It was a timber town of
intensive cutting; it was a cattle town where for generations
the cattle had ravaged the land; it was a mining town in which
I could see the scarred landscape around me. I grew up in a culture that celebrated the evidence of individual accomplishment,
that was certain death to the sound and the mystery and the
romance of the land.

I went away to college in the late 1950s to study science, really
because I think I had soaked up this tradition and saw science

as the tool by which to complete the conquest of the West,
a way of infusing some extra power into the mythology that
I had grown up in. A science professor of mine handed me a
book with the odd title *Beyond the Hundredth Meridian,* and as
I read it, it was as if somebody had thrown a rock through a
windowpane, a rock that landed in the middle of the edifice
built up around me for a great many years. Because I suddenly
saw an entirely different landscape; I saw an entirely different
culture; I saw a history of conflict and destruction; and I mar-
velled at an interpretation that I had never dreamed of. It had
never been presented to me anywhere in the culture that I grew
up in. Wallace Stegner's analysis of what had happened to the
American West culminated in a description that guides me to
this day, as I now take my turn in the dramatic interaction between the western mythology of individualism and the see-saw
struggle with other partnerships and communities . . . and yes,
even with government, something that was an unthinkable possi-
bility when I grew up on the land, taught to hate the U.S. Forest
Service, to see the Bureau of Land Management as an oppressor
upon the land.

The culminating moment in Stegner's description of this in-
terplay between the two western traditions, the solid mythology
of individualism and the oncoming possibilities of community
and partnership, occurred in the 1880s. His description of this
moment, the way he unearthed this from archives of history and
held it up to me and to a whole generation, was an astounding
fact. What he showed us was that in the presence of John Wesley
Powell, and in the presence of a small book called *Report on the
Arid Region of the United States,* written in the 1880s, there was
another vision of the West. Stegner went on to describe the first
test between these two possibilities. It came in the 1880s as John
Wesley Powell's view of the West, and his understanding of the
limitations imposed by the aridity of the land and the need for

human institutions that could respond in a mode of cooperation, came all the way up to Washington, to the U.S. Congress. It resulted in one striking moment, the creation of something called the U.S. Irrigation Survey, which for one or two seasons suspended all the homestead and land entry laws in the West and put the U.S. government behind the proposition that the scientists and the visionaries would lead the way west and would enter into a partnership to decide where the land could and should be settled, and the type of institutions that would be necessary to bring water to the land, and the way in which we might find a sort of symbiosis, a way that we could live intelligently and lightly on the land. Stegner then recounted how it all came to an abrupt and shattering end, as the mythical West rose up through its political representatives in the U.S. Congress and drove Powell off the face of the land.

And I've thought about that often since, because don't you see? Don't you see? You know, that's a lot of people, that's some of my predecessors: Albert Fall, Jim Watt, and others. It's a story that has been repeated generation after generation, a story that is still going on, because we have never yet succeeded in finding that balance. Stegner's pulling that artifact up from history and showing us its context provided me in that moment a way of thinking differently about the West. I went back and reread *Beyond the Hundredth Meridian* the week after I took office and thought, Yes, it's as true now as it was true then, the outcome is still very much in the balance, the forces are the same. Not much has changed in a hundred years. The stakes have gotten higher, because there aren't as many empty spaces, there are more people, more pressure, more demand for the resources. But in that one book, and in his way of looking at the West, Stegner leaves us a message that the duality, the tensions have never been resolved. Each generation is once again given the chance to see if it can't somehow find that balance and realign its view of the land, its relationship with the land, and the way that our institutions can be put into the mix, not as adversaries, but as part of a broader community.

Burning Sage
at the Department
of Interior

Terry Tempest Williams

Remarks in remembrance of Wallace Stegner,
delivered at the Interior South Building,
Washington, D.C., April 22, 1993

ONCE WHEN I WAS IN TROUBLE with the Mormon Church,
Wally wrote me a letter. We had discussed the difficulty of a
free voice in Zion. His letter read something like, "Consider
me your patriarch now. Whatever blessings you are in need
of I will shower upon you. I am your elder." He will forever be.

The last time Wally and Mary Stegner were in Utah, the home
Wally adopted in his heart and the home that I was born to, he
filled me with a roving and lyrical narrative, an annotated drive,
really, through the town and adjacent desert that he loved. We
passed the place where he and my grandfather had played tennis in the twenties, where he took his first date for ice cream.
He suggested that we stop, the three of us, and have milkshakes,
but Mary reminded him that the plane was leaving shortly.

And then we came to the area where *Recapitulation* was set.
We rolled down the windows of the car—it had just rained—
and we all took deep breaths. Sage. The sweet smell from the
foothills filled every cell in our bodies. It took our breath all the
way down. It was the West. It was home. "An acquired taste,"
Wally said.

When it was time for the Stegners to leave, we arrived at the airport, and I helped carry some of their luggage to the ticket counter. As they boarded the plane, I turned to Wally and said, "Thank you so much for coming." He faced me dead center and said, "Thank you for staying."

I would like to extend that same sentiment to you, to those of you in the Department of Interior, and thank you for staying, for weathering the past twelve years. I know it hasn't been easy. And for those of you, those of us, in the conservation community, thank you for staying, for having the staying power that Wallace Stegner so admired. I believe there are warriors in this room.

I would also like to honor Secretary Babbitt, for his innovations and his depth of soul, in gathering us together in the name of family, to honor one of our elders. I love that this governing agency that is the overseer and caretaker of our public lands is called Department of Interior. Interior—think about it—where the heart lies. Conscience; reflection; interior. I would like to suggest that the bridge between the interior world and the exterior world is story. And no one knew that more powerfully than Wally.

The story "Genesis," in Wally's book *Wolf Willow,* if you remember, is a story about a company of cow punchers who are engaged in a cattle drive in Saskatchewan. They are caught in a blizzard that covers and exposes human frailties and character. At one point the protagonist, Rusty, steps out of the line cabin:

The big pale earth was around him, the big mottled sky arched over with a slice of very white moon shining on icy-looking clouds. It was so quiet he heard his own heart thudding. For a moment he stood taking it in, and then he opened his mouth and let out a very loud yell, simply to announce himself and to crack the silence. When he went back in, hissing and shaking, he found them all staring at him.

"What in hell was that?" Buck said.

"That was me," Rusty said. "It was too quiet to suit me."

"He was young and susceptible, but he was probably not far wrong in his feeling that there never was a lonelier land,"

Stegner continues to write, "and one in which men lived more uneasily on sufferance. And he thought he knew the answer to the challenge Saskatchewan tossed him: to be invincibly strong, indefinitely enduring, uncompromisingly self-reliant, to depend on no one, to contain within himself every strength and every skill."

As this two-week cattle drive continues, and as they face this storm, at one point Wally says that Rusty and Spurlock, these two men who are holding each other, literally, are two corpses facing the inevitability of their lives:

the Rusty Cullen who sat among them was a different boy, outside, inside, from the one who had set out with them two weeks before. He thought that he knew enough not to want to distinguish himself by heroic deeds: single-handed walks to the North Pole, incredible journeys, rescues, what-not. Given his way, he did not think that he would ever want to do anything alone again, not in this country. Even a trip to the privy was something a man might want to take in company.

The notion insinuated itself into his head, not for the first time, that his sticking with Spurlock after Panguingue left was an act of special excellence, that the others must look upon him with a new respect because of it. But the tempting thought did not stand up under the examination he gave it. Special excellence? Why hadn't anyone praised him for it, then? He knew why: because it was what any of them would have done. To have done less would have been cowardice and disgrace. It was probably a step in the making of a cowhand when he learned that what would pass for heroics in a softer world was only chores around here.

What I can tell you about this story is that Wally was scheduled to read it for Audio Press in June. His request. He called them. "I want this story out in the world," he said. Why? Why *this* story? Why "Genesis"? Of all his work? Because it is about the rugged individualism of the American West transformed into partnership, about tender caring for one another, about the simple common decency between human beings.

In Utah, as in so many places in this country, this is exactly the story we need to be telling. In his novel *Crossing to Safety,* a story

of friendship between Larry and Sally Morgan, Sid and Charity
Lang, Wally writes,

*What ever happened to the passion we all had to improve ourselves, live
up to our potential, leave a mark on the world? Our hottest arguments
were always about how we could* contribute. *We did not care about the
rewards. We were young and earnest. We never kidded ourselves that we
had the political gifts to reorder society or insure social justice. . . . But
we all hoped, in whatever way our capacities permitted, to define and
illustrate the worthy life.*

And a hundred pages later, a ceremony:

Whup! *his cork hits the ceiling.* Whup! *Mine follows. Cheers. People drain
their glasses, and hold their empties toward us, and we pour. Then Sid is lifting his glass and calling for quiet. Finally he gets it. Sally, I see, is back on the
couch. I move to get to her with the champagne bottle, but she raises her glass
to show me that someone has already provided.*

*"To the talent in our midst," Sid says. "To the marriage of match and
kindling, the divine oxidation."*

May we utter this same kind of toast here. And set the Department of Interior on fire. Ignite our country in the pursuit
of liberty, which is the pursuit of wildness, raw and self-defined.
Consider your birthright, Stegner tells us, when fatigue or lazi-
ness threatens to slow our hungry slurping of culture, think who
you are. Perhaps the greatest legacy that Wally has taught us is
that our birthright is found in the land, in wilderness, in the geography of hope. Genesis, match and kindling, sage. Words of sage.
Stegner, our sage. His life, his words, bind us together as a community of friends and family engaged in a vision. Let us regard
the land as holy. Let us regard the land as sacred. They are our
sacrament. Blood, body, sage. Let us breathe deeply. Thank you
for staying.

Wallace Stegner and the Rigor of Civility

Charles Wilkinson

Remarks in remembrance of Wallace Stegner,
delivered at the Interior South Building,
in Washington, D.C., April 22, 1993

IN 1984, I WAS JUST GETTING STARTED on a book on the
West. For more than a decade before that, my thinking had
been lifted by the wind currents of *Beyond the Hundredth Meridian*, *The Big Rock Candy Mountain*, *Wolf Willow*, *The Sound of Mountain Water*, and *Angle of Repose*, and I wanted to talk about this
new venture, right at the beginning, before the book took shape,
with Wallace Stegner.

But how would you go *about* meeting with Wallace Stegner?

On an impulse, I wrote him a letter, almost a formal proposal, really, enclosing a couple of my articles and asking
for an audience. I told my wife, Ann, I'd done this and then
promptly forgot about it. A meeting with Wallace Stegner?
He'd never even reply.

I took off on a trip and, on the way back, stopped over in
Quincy, California, in the Sierra, with Jean Cunningham's
family. Jean is Ann's sister and the Cunninghams are blood

relatives all the way. In the morning I called home, talked awhile
with Ann, and was getting ready to say good-bye when Ann said,
with studied casualness, as I think she would admit, "Oh, by the
way. You got a letter from Wallace Stegner."

I remember where I was standing, how the early sun slanted
through the bay window, how the Cunningham kids were scuf-
fling around on the sofa, and the way thoughts were clanging
around in my head—the one I remember best being, "Can't be.
I wrote him just four days ago."

"Ann, open it. Tell me what it says."

Ann, who I don't believe had ever opened a single letter of
mine, replied, "I already have."

"What did he say?"

"He said he would love to meet with you any time you want.
He says he has time on his hands. Listen to this."

Ann then read me this passage, which I will pass on, not from
memory, but from my Wallace Stegner file, the first time I'd ever
set up a file just for a person:

How can we get together? I'll be here [in California], *with minor excursions
of a few days to a week, until about mid-June. Then I'm going to Vermont
again, with a carload of books and xeroxed authorities, to brood from a distance about the West. Will you be in the East at all this summer? Our summer
address is simply Greensboro, Vermont (Justice Rehnquist's too, if you're interested). Our telephone number there is (802) 533-7010. If you're anywhere
close, it would be a great privilege to talk to you. Our own cottage is more like
a shack, but we can find you a primitive bed and plenty to eat; or we can get
you a room at the local inn. In case you're coming through the Bay Area
before we leave, it's easier and somewhat less spartan.*

I had inadvertently uncovered one of the sweetest blessings
of the world, which I kept a secret—theoretically out of respect
for his privacy but actually out of pure selfishness—which is
that Wally Stegner would answer any letter, right now, peck-
ing away on a clunker of a typewriter that was probably used,

secondhand, by someone of John Wesley Powell's, Helen Hunt Jackson's, or Brigham Young's vintage. And those letters were literate and invariably funny.

Once I sent him one of my speeches, in which I had tried in a frail way to explain Wally's influence. He and Mary had been on vacation and he hadn't gotten to his mail. His opening line was: "I cost myself two weeks of self-satisfaction and smugness by not getting around to your lecture earlier."

It tickled me when in another letter he discussed the topic I'd written him on, answered my question, and then, with a flick of his mind, changed the subject by beginning the next paragraph with: "While I've got you on the line . . ."

He regularly complained about his growing number of ailments—the only pale solace we can take is that though he seemed strong to us, he hated the ravages of time, and, in his mind, he was ready. But he was philosophical about this, always with a twinkle in his eye. This three years ago:

I'm typing with one finger of one hand because walking with a cane has bug-gered up my left wrist. Please forgive typos. The slower I go the more typos I make. Maybe when that new hip is in place I'll even recover the use of my hands, and will stand before you transfigured, restored to my youthful vigor, ready for fun or frolic.

Over those years, he gave me so much. That May, that slow, easy brunch on the deck, Wally and Mary, sweethearts for fifty-nine years, all manner of rambling conversation topics. It seemed without end, still does. The big-moon, lakeside talk, when I finally dared to ask about *The Big Rock Candy Mountain*. My own father had been hard on me. The passages about the humiliation the father had given the boy in the book, which I knew to be generally autobiographical, were they true? "Yes, yes they were. Just like it's written." So Wally had made it. So could I.

Out on a hike in Montana, I recalled an old article, where he had mentioned taking Page camping while he was out on the Colorado Plateau working on the Powell book. I told him that the idea took hold with me, and that I brought a boy with me whenever I could and that it was one of my joys. "I'm glad," he said. "I didn't realize it would have that impact on anyone." He looked up the trail and I could see the inlaid humility grudgingly giving way, once again, to his own private wonder that a boy from nowhere could send out so many messages of so many sorts to so many people in so many places.

The life's work that Wally wove was so large, the designs so intricate and the natural colors so many, that you do not try to encapsulate it or boil it down. One main part of the pattern, though, involved civility. The kindness and gentleness expressed in his correspondence and conversations were testament to his belief in individual responsibility, to his conviction that, out of respect for the humanity of others, a person—and a society—ought to be civil. But there was an edge to this, for Wally made it clear that there are consequences when civility is absent.

He knew the incivility—the cruelty—that tears a society because he saw it and sometimes helped cause it. Of East End, Saskatchewan—the Whitemud of *Wolf Willow*—which he loved, along with Salt Lake City, the most, simply because he lived there the longest and became most settled and organic with the place, he confessed this:

The folk culture sponsored every sort of crude practical joke, as it permitted the cruelest and ugliest prejudices and persecutions. Any visible difference was enough to get an individual picked on. Impartially and systematically we persecuted Mah Li and his brother Mah Jim, Jew Meyer and his family, any Indians who came down into the valley in their wobble-wheeled buckboards, anyone with a pronounced English accent or fancy clothes or affected manners, any child with glasses, anyone afflicted with crossed eyes, St. Vitus's dance, feeble-mindedness, or a game leg. Systematically the strong bullied the weak, and the weak did their best to persuade their persecutors, by feats of courage or endurance or by picking on someone still weaker, that they were tough and strong. (Wolf Willow)

He wrote often of the effort it takes to make civility in the American West. Many of these were miscellaneous events, for miscellany is a tight-woven society's wool. In "Genesis," his epic story of the Northern Plains' bitter winter of 1906, a story of beginnings and endings that he wanted to read for audio tape before his own ending, but never did, he wrote of Rusty Cullen, "a different boy, inside and outside, from the one who had set out with them two weeks before." Rusty, who had stuck with Spurlock during the killing storm, found himself wondering why no one mentioned his heroic deeds:

Special excellence? Why hadn't anyone praised him for it, then? He knew why: because it was what any of them would have done. To have done less would have been cowardice and disgrace. It was probably a step in the making of a cowhand when he learned that what would pass for heroics in a softer world was only chores around here. (Wolf Willow)

Wally believed that women had done a big part of the good work. His mother made him feel worthy, and that worthiness allowed him to withstand his father's batterings. She was a hero in his novels and in his life. In his work on the Mormons, both admiring and critical, I found the most telling observation of all to be a well-placed sentence from *The Gathering of Zion*: "Their women," he wrote, "were incredible."

The Mormon practice of community was embedded in his work in many ways, but nowhere more specifically than with Powell. The second expedition laid over in Kanab for the winter of 1871. Powell had brought Emma, and three-month-old Mary, down from Salt Lake City. Stegner wrote:

[The expedition's] *camp was at Eight Mile Spring, their entertainment the dances in the Kanab branch ward house and an occasional jug of wine made*

in the Mormon "Dixie" around St. George. For a while, with the ladies, the
baby, the dances, the contacts with the gawky Mormon girls, leathery patri-
archs, credulous and hardy young men, "aunties" with broods but without
visible husbands, the Powell Expedition had a reasonably social time.
(Beyond the Hundredth Meridian)

The experience took. In 1878, when Powell wrote his report on the arid lands of the West (it was Stegner's plan, too),
Powell built on the Mormons' belief in, and practice of,
civic cooperation:

The Mormons of Kanab and the Sevier Valley towns had taught him more
than irrigation. From them he had also got a notion of how salutary coop-
eration could be as a way of life, how much less wasteful than competition
unlimited, how much more susceptible to planning and intelligence, how
much less destructive of human and natural resources. The last step of
his proposal . . . embodied official encouragement of a social organiza-
tion thoroughly revolutionary in 1878. It was so far beyond the social
and economic thinking of the period that popularized the pork barrel
as a national symbol and began the systematic gutting of the continent's
resources and developed to its highest and most ruthless stage the compet-
itive ruthlessness of American business, that [the Powell and Mormon
ideal] *seems like the product of another land and another people.* (Beyond
the Hundredth Meridian)

Wally's principles required him both to live his life that civil,
gentle way and to expect it of others. It was a demanding code.
He breathed fire over every massacre of Indians that could have
been prevented by slowing down and taking the time to sort out
the cultural differences; every dam that could have been obviated
by decent conservation practices; every road cut into wild country for a few board feet that could have been harvested elsewhere
as second growth, if we had just restocked instead of cutting and
running; every child dislodged from her or his own soil when the
bust, bred of a big-eyed boom, crowbarred the family out and on
to a new town. How, one of his largest questions was, could a civilized society do such things?

His ideas about the rigor of civility became so formidable because his thinking and writing were themselves so rigorous. Though never trained as a historian, Wally took up the profession's best tools and put them to heavy labor. He went to primary documents; he looked to his own life experiences, for he lived the West from wild land to the plow to the city; he got his facts meticulously right; he wove together accurate facts involving different places, people, and events; then, having set the record straight, an action he saw as the roadbed for progress, he articulated large and lasting warnings and lessons from that history. The results were at once so careful and so full. As Page Stegner rightly explained it, "He had a kind of holistic relationship with the land, and he couldn't look at it without remembering its geological history, its exploration, its social development, its contemporary problems, and its prognosis for the future." And the level of prose that the keys of that old typing machine pecked off, well. . . .

In 1991, Wally wrote an op-ed piece in the *Los Angeles Times* on water—a strong, lyrical, concise, no-nonsense piece. Vintage Stegner. At the end, he said, "We need a redeemer." We need, he wrote, someone to make western water right and, by clear extension, make the West right.

Now we fully know. We've had our redeemer. There can never be another like him, and now the work is left to the daughters and sons of Wallace Stegner. That surely includes those of us here in this perfectly symbolic place, within the government department that can do the most for the arid West, for the canyon and plateau country that Wally loved so, where the views, as he wrote, "fill up the eye and overflow the soul." Yes, it is left to us, and those of us in many other places, to carry on the work of our gracious, elegant, demanding redeemer.

Many of you will know the words I plan to read last. But they are like Shakespeare, Beethoven, or Picasso: it is good to return, to pull once more the dog-eared *Lear* from the shelf; to settle deeply into a seat in the music hall for another Ninth; to walk again the hallways of the Prado. This is for us, Wally's daughters and sons:

Angry as one may be at what heedless men have done and still do to a noble habitat, one cannot be pessimistic about the West. This is the native home of hope. When it fully learns that cooperation, not rugged individualism, is the quality that most characterizes and preserves it, then it will have achieved itself and outlived its origins. Then it has a chance to create a society to match its scenery. (The Sound of Mountain Water)

Letter
to Mary

T. H. Watkins

THIS IS A DREADFULLY HARD letter to write, as I'm sure you understand (and which explains my delay in writing it). I want somehow to pull together in one place words of comfort, words of pain, words of appreciation, words of love, and it probably cannot be done. You know everything I am going to say, and much much more, but I hope you will forgive me if I babble on anyway.

It is, first of all, impertinent of me even to suggest I know how you feel right now. How could I possibly know the measure of your loss? So I will say no such thing. Better I should just forward my love, for whatever comfort it offers, then say what I think the rest of us have lost in the death of someone of Wally's stature— the loss being measured by the dimensions of what he gave while he was with us.

Those of us who were fortunate enough to have known Wallace Stegner have lost someone who stood at the center of our personal world—unassumingly and sometimes, I think, not really aware of the position he occupied in our lives. We remember him as a man of extraordinary inner grace, one who lived out in his own life the dictum he laid down as one of the proper functions of literature: character revealed through action. The character the action of his life revealed was one of inherent gentleness, intellectual depth, personal integrity, puckish humor, great kindness, generosity of spirit, and, above all, a stubborn conviction that we must all treat one another with love, kindness, dignity, and respect—though when righteous anger is called for, we should have the gumption to stand up and declare it.

When another old friend of mine, historian W. H. Hutchinson, died in 1990, Wally wrote to express his sympathy and to say that about the best you could hope for when departing this cooling cinder was that the good you had done while here managed to outweigh the bad—and that he was sure old Hutch had tipped the scales pretty heavily in the right direction. For Wally, I think, they haven't yet built scales capable of holding the weight of his good.

I am not talking here just about personal good, for all its abundance in him. I am talking about the character of his contribution to the literary and intellectual fabric of the Republic over a career that spanned nearly sixty years. It was not a public career in the sense we have come to know (and abuse) the term; he gave up only that part of himself he believed the public needed to know in order to understand his work and his causes. At the same time, he was no recluse squatting in a cave, contemplating the lambent significance of his personal navel. He believed deeply in the necessity of true *civitas*, that it is one of the primary obligations of citizenship to participate in the function of government, especially when one holds a position of influence, even when it interferes with what he would much rather have been doing—writing—which it did quite a lot of the time.

Nor did he define himself narrowly. We know him, most of us, mainly from his fiction, but time already has judged him one of the country's most significant historians. He was, of course, a teacher, an alumnus of the faculty of the famous Bread Loaf Writer's Conference in Vermont, and for twenty-five years head of the Creative Writing Program he founded at Stanford. As essays in the old *Saturday Review of Literature* and many other publications demonstrated, he was an incisive and intelligent critic of the work of others, from A. B. Guthrie to Anne Tyler. It is less well known that he also was a first-class journalist when he put his mind to it—as he did to wonderful effect in such books as

Mormon Country and *One Nation.* He was even, for a few years, an editor—heading up the staff of *The American West,* a magazine that for a while attempted to do for the West what *American Heritage* did for the nation as a whole—bring literary respectability to popular history.

Nancy Packer, his friend and successor as head of the Stanford Writing Program, called him one of modern America's few genuine "belletrists," a true man of letters. If that description applies, and I think it does, he also may have been the only such individual whose voice had its roots, but not its limits, in the great ill-defined vastness we call the West—ill defined because it was and is, as Archibald MacLeish pointed out, a "country in the mind."

It certainly was a country firmly fixed in Stegner's mind and work. Just as surely as the western experience helped to shape us as a nation, it informed the spirit and intellect of his writing. It was neither a casual nor a superficial influence; it had little to do with cowboys and even less with Indians, at least as our myths have twisted both beyond recognition. The influence ran deep, down to the marrow where imagination lies, and was all of a piece with the man. No other major modern writer knew so much of the West from personal experience, none so steeped himself in its history, and none did so much with what he found in both.

From that coherence of personal experience, intellectual inquiry, and creative expression, Wallace Stegner gave those of us who came to maturity in the West something precious: he gave us our history, our true history, not the mindless natterings of literary con artists who exploit it or the stubborn ignorance of eastern historians who simply will not understand its importance. No one, not even Bernard DeVoto, wrote more intelligently or forcefully or effectively about the true nature of a history lived out in an arid land, of both its delight and its sorrow, its potential and its limits. From *Beyond the Hundredth Meridian,* his 1954 biography of explorer and practical visionary John Wesley Powell, to *Where the Bluebird Sings to the Lemonade Springs,* his

1992 collection of essays, Wally cut into the essence of the western experience, laying bare its often grotesque excesses without once losing sight of the fact that, as he put it, the West was still "the native home of hope."

The West also figures importantly, though not exclusively, in the best of the fiction he gave us, from the still-powerful *Big Rock Candy Mountain* of 1943 to the prize-winning *Angle of Repose* of 1971—not to mention the dozens of short stories that placed him on a plane with John Cheever and other masters of the form, even if the literary mafia that resides east of the Hudson River could never quite bring itself to recognize the fact. It hasn't been that long, after all, since *The New York Times Magazine* somehow managed to run a photograph of Wally, proudly identifying him as *William* Stegner.

I don't feel competent to discuss Stegner's fiction in literary terms, having neither experience as a critic nor talent as a fictionist. I cheerfully assert, however, that the great bulk of this work will remain one of the most important interpretations we have ever had of the past and present condition of life in this nation— and a beacon of honesty lighting the dark, twisty, endlessly surprising passageways of the human mind and heart. Norman Cousins once said that the quality that most accurately characterized Stegner's fiction was its integrity. Wally did not often write about what he had not known and experienced himself, and always regretted the attempt when he tried—as in *Fire and Ice,* the one book of his I think he believed to be a failure. If so, the rest of his fictional work, devoid of trickery, as implacably honest as he knew how to make it, no matter the pain he may have experienced in the process, rises like the Front Range of the Rockies in the semiarid plain of twentieth-century American literature.

What Stegner gave us in history and in fiction are legacies to be cherished, God knows. But there is something else, something that the world of conservation is especially privileged to share.

When his old friend and mentor Bernard DeVoto died in 1955, Wally said that one big question arose in the minds of those who had known him: "Who will do his work?" In the midst of the hurt we feel at Stegner's death, the same sad insistent question lingers, though with a different inflection now: who will do *his* work?

Not that Wally himself would have accepted the query as entirely legitimate. He always had trouble understanding just how necessary he was. When I accused him once of being one of the most important figures in the modern conservation movement, he refused to let me put him on a pedestal with such activists as Howard Zahniser of The Wilderness Society or David Brower of the Sierra Club. "I am a paper tiger, Watkins," he wrote, "typewritten on both sides."

That, though he was reluctant to admit it, was exactly the point. It is quite impossible to think of the long struggle for conservation without conjuring up a pantheon of names, from Henry David Thoreau to Edward Abbey, whose illumination has provided the very light by which we work. Wally was not only firmly fixed at the highest level of this tradition, he became one of the most eloquent and intelligent voices in defense of the voiceless that our literature has ever produced.

From the wind-blasted plains of Saskatchewan to the glorious canyon country of southern Utah, from the alpine lakes and meadows of the Rockies to the basin-and-range deserts of Nevada, from California's Coast Ranges to Vermont's hills and hollows, Wally repeatedly celebrated the land and its community of life. From that abundant well of experience and love he gave us not merely the taste and look and feel of the land he wrote about so wonderfully, but in both fiction and nonfiction he kept reminding us, over and over with quiet, eloquent insistence, branding it into our minds with unforgettable language, that without the land and the wild creatures in it, we were nothing, ciphers with brains, clever stick-people without a future.

They were sometimes angry, those writings. Sabrina Castro, the heroine of his 1961 novel *A Shooting Star*, for example, was not speaking independently of her maker, after all, when she ruminated about her brother, a real-estate developer:

His kind never anticipated consequences. His was the kind that left eroded gulches and cutover timberlands and man-made deserts and jerry-built tracts that would turn into slums in less than a generation. . . . They denuded and uglified the earth in the name of progress, and when they lay in their deathbeds—or dropped from the massive coronary that the pace of their lives prepared for them—they were buried full of honors and rolling in wealth, and it never occurred to the people who honored them, any more than it had occurred to themselves, that they nearly always left the earth poorer and drearier for their having lived in it.

For intensity of feeling, I will put that up against any yelp of outrage that would later erupt from Stegner's old student, Ed Abbey. But, like Abbey, I will concede, even when driven by wrath, Wally's words were never just the artless polemics of a conservation writer; they were the declarations of an oracle—or a prophet speaking from the heart of the desert he loved so much. He would scoff and aim a kick at my shins if he could hear that, but it is true nevertheless. Wally spent his days building a great architecture of words, like a craftsman painstakingly assembling the pieces of a wonderful building. He then gave it the breath of art, and with that glorious exhalation, the limitless power of pure understanding. And it is perhaps a measure of his love that in no other single piece of writing from a long career did he achieve such majesty of language as in his famous "Wilderness Letter" of 1960. It may have been just "the labor of an afternoon," as he once said, but it has long since become one of the central documents in the history of the conservation movement: "Something will have gone out of us as a people," he wrote,

if we ever let the remaining wilderness be destroyed; if we permit the last virgin forests to be turned into comic books and plastic cigarette cases; if we drive the few remaining members of the wild species into zoos or to extinction; if we pollute the last clear air and dirty the last clean streams and push our paved roads through the last of the silence, so that never again will Americans be free in their own country from the noise, the exhausts, the stinks of human and automotive waste. And so that never again can we have the chance to see ourselves single, separate, vertical and individual in the world, part of the environment of trees and rocks and soil, brother to the other animals, part of the natural world and competent to belong in it. . . .

We simply need that wild country available to us, even if we never do more than drive to its edge and look in. For it can be a means of reassuring ourselves of our sanity as creatures, a part of the geography of hope.

Altogether, then, Wally's legacy to the nation in his writings over a career that spanned sixty years is one of those treasures that validates our history as a people, and because of it he has provided himself with a species of immortality.

Those of us left behind, of course, would prefer something closer to the real thing, because there is a sudden and irreparable vacancy in our lives. Certainly in mine. I once told Wally that one of the most endearing things about him, in my experience, was that from the first moment we met back in 1966 he treated me with the quiet deference of an "equal." To understand the importance of this to me, you have to know that when we met I still was bundling up newspapers for a living, had never taken a course in creative writing, had published nothing but a few profoundly insignificant book reviews and a couple of very, very minor articles, and was stupefyingly callow.

I pranced about him like an overgrown—and overblown—puppy, offering up mindless comments on sundry aspects of his work and what I perceived to be the true meaning of literature, and he treated me with attentive respect instead of the disdain I so richly deserved. He nodded sagely in agreement with my judgments, thanked me sincerely for my praise, said kind things about my own bush league efforts, and encouraged me to commit more of them. If I had not revered him before, I sure did then.

I never really lost that first astonished wonder, and I'm sure it embarrassed Wally on more than one occasion. Not that he would ever have said so. The only indication he ever gave that he thought I might be acting like an idiot at any given moment was an occasional facial twitch of what I am sure now was a kind of affectionate amusement. I treasure those moments, too.

I think every writer has someone specific for whom he writes, that person whose presence can be felt just over the left shoulder as he works. I don't know whose presence stood behind Wally's chair, but I know that for more than a quarter of a century, Wally stood behind mine. What I wrote and how it appeared on the page were influenced by the invisible presence of his judgment. I am going to miss that presence more than I can possibly say. Who am I writing for now?

That is only one part of him that I will miss. The long conversation of our correspondence was one of the great joys of my life; every time I pawed through my mail and found a letter from him, there was then nothing that could happen in that day that could hope to depress me. The humor, cheerful skepticism, abiding affection, and, yes, beGod, wisdom of those letters constitute a library into which I still dip for inspiration and guidance. They almost make up for the fact that for my money we never did have enough time together. This was my own doing, I fear. Like a careless son, I spent too much time thinking I would have plenty of time. I remember every single one of the occasions when we were together, though, particularly those times we sat on his deck overlooking the lion-colored flanks of California's summer hills. These remain in my memory like impossibly luminous moments, like Camelots.

I loved him, of course, though I never fully understood how much and never got up the nerve to tell him. I hope he knew, though. A great part of the center of my life has been taken from me, and I am left spinning, without a reference point for much of my thoughts and feelings. I know that this sudden rootlessness will pass, or at least I hope it does, but I also know that for twenty-seven years I was privileged to dance in the shadow of greatness and that for the rest of my own life I will carry his memory like a nimbus.

The Momentum
of Clarity
Wendell Berry

FOR A LONG TIME, whenever I have thought about Wallace
Stegner and his work, I have always come up against the need
to make sense of the way influence works within a culture, and
my thoughts have always proceeded from that need to a mixture
of wonder and confusion. It is nevertheless impossible for me
to talk about this man, who for me has been a landmark, without addressing somehow this issue of influence. I will have to
address it by way of a little bit of autobiography, and I ask your
pardon for this.

I came to Stanford as a fellow in the writing program in the fall
of 1958. The seminar in the Jones Room of the library was ably
and kindly taught that fall by Richard Scowcroft, and the next
spring we continued with Wallace Stegner. Though I remain certain in memory and feeling of the impression this Mr. Stegner
made on me, I have a hard time describing it, perhaps because
he was not in any sense a "type." He was a fine-looking man of
about fifty, gray-haired, courteous, generous, smiling (though
perhaps not at something we knew), neatly and even elegantly
but never ostentatiously dressed; sometimes, as the class carried
on its business of reading and talking, he would smoke medita-
tively a cigar. He did not seem to be a professor at all, and when
he was in it the Jones Room did not seem part of a school. He
had, of course, *been* to school, but one could tell that to a very
considerable extent he had not been *made* by school. He managed somehow to imply that the work and the interest that had
brought us together were matters in some respects practical. He

did not deal in infallible recipes, or guarantee results. He did not suggest that all our problems were solvable. But there was in his presence and bearing the implication that we could work at our problems, and that we should. I thought, and think still, that he was a good teacher. When I sit at my worktable now I am aware of certain attitudes, hesitations, and insistences that I think are traceable to that seminar thirty-four years ago.

I wish I could say that I then understood him as an influence— that I saw what he was about, or saw how to apply his example to my own life. But the fact is that at that time I did not understand him as an influence, and the reason was that at that time I did not know what kind of influence I was going to need. At that time I only wanted to be a writer; beyond that, I had little self-knowledge, and not an inkling of what I wanted to do or where I wanted to do it. I was living outside my life.

I got back inside my life in 1964 when I returned to my own part of the country. From that time I began a long and still-continuing process of understanding Wallace Stegner as an influence, and of being influenced by him. But here again I am embarrassed. As I failed to understand him as an influence when I first knew him, so have I failed to know very exactly how his influence has grown upon me; it has been involved in my life as I have lived it.

The difficulty is increased by my inability to separate the influence of the books from the influence of the man himself. Behind the books, for me, has been the presence of a man I would have liked and admired if he had not written a word. And I should add that, to Tanya and me, it has mattered inestimably that he and Mary so obviously and significantly mattered to one another.

Beginning with *A Shooting Star* in 1961, I read Wally's books as they came out. In 1962 he published *Wolf Willow*, and I remember clearly my happiness in reading it. With that book, I began to see that side by side with his interest in the West as the subject of his stories and novels was an interest in the West as a place, a living place, *his* living place—and a place, moreover, that had been grossly misunderstood in the course of white settlement and was therefore gravely in need of a complex protection, "a civilization to match its scenery."

Eventually I thought there must have been a moment when he decided that he would not be the kind of writer who would look on his native country as "raw material" for his art, and leave it otherwise to take care of itself or to be cared for by other people, but that he would be a kind of writer who would be devoted to his country for its own sake, and do what he could to protect it. And then I thought that perhaps he had not decided—that perhaps there had come a moment, simply, when he realized that he had become that second kind of writer. Whenever and however that moment occurred, it was a significant moment; so far as I know, no American storyteller had been that kind of writer before.

He became the man and the writer he became, of course, because he had entered a web of influence that inclined him to be what he became. The primary influence undoubtedly was his long and intimate knowledge of the country itself, but he acknowledged also the influence of human predecessors. In his conversations with Richard Etulain, for example, he said, "Powell taught Webb . . . Powell and Webb, between them, taught Benny DeVoto, and they all taught me." He became an influence, then, partly because he had *accepted* an influence. I entered the same web of influence at a later time and from a different part of the country, but with his work in mind—and when I did finally enter it Wallace Stegner became my teacher in a way much more profound and useful than before. But "teacher" is not quite the proper word, nor even is "influence" in the usual sense. For he and his work were becoming part of my mind, what I had to think and respond with.

After Edward Abbey died in the spring of 1989, many of his friends met to honor him in the desert near Moab, Utah. Wally, who could not attend, sent a letter to be read at the gathering. In it, he said of Ed Abbey, who had been his student, "He was a red hot moment in the conscience of the country." Wallace Stegner too was a moment in the country's conscience—not a red hot moment, but one that was luminous, clarifying, and steady. The word "moment" suggests no dispraise in either case, for these are moments outside of time that can be returned to; the word suggests only that such illuminations occur in a lineage or web of lineages that grows as it continues.

We speak naturally, and I think accurately, of a "web of influence," but it is perhaps useful to change the metaphor by thinking of this influence literally as a flow: a steadily augmenting flow of consciousness and of conscience moving toward our country, the American land itself. One enters this flow by way of a "moment" (a *momentum*) of clarity instinct with the power to ignite other such moments.

It is pleasing and reassuring to remember the care that Wally took to understand himself as part of this still-building influence. As readily as he acknowledged his predecessors, he credited his contemporaries and successors. He was always a giver, never a taker, of credit. In the introduction to his last book of essays, he wrote,

looking at the western writers, not only the ones I will discuss here [John Steinbeck, George R. Stewart, Walter Van Tilburg Clark, and Norman Maclean], but all the new ones, the Ivan Doigs and Bill Kittredges and James Welches, the Gretel Ehrlichs and Rudolfo Anayas and John Daniels, the Scott Momadays and Louise Erdrichs and many more, I feel the surge of the inextinguishable western hope. It is a civilization they are building, a history they are compiling, a way of looking at the world and humanity's place in it. I think they will do it. . . . It has already begun.

At first, reading that passage, one may take it to be merely characteristic of his generosity. But then one sees that its governing pronoun is "they": "It is a civilization *they* are building. . . . I think *they* will do it." Not many writers, and not many people, have evolved from "I" through "we" to this freely affirmed and welcomed "they." And how moving it is, after looking twice, to see in this almost unnoticeable self-effacement the fineness, the magnanimity, and something of the greatness of Wallace Stegner.

The Cultivated Wild
of Wallace Stegner
John Daniel

*Something will have gone out of us as a people if we ever
let the remaining wilderness be destroyed; if we permit the
last virgin forests to be turned into comic books and plastic
cigarette cases; if we drive the few remaining members of the
wild species into zoos or to extinction; if we pollute the last
clear air and dirty the last clean streams and push our paved
roads through the last of the silence, so that never again will
Americans be free in their own country from the noise, the
exhausts, the stinks of human and automotive waste. And
so that never again can we have the chance to see ourselves
single, separate, vertical and individual in the world, part
of the environment of trees and rocks and soil, brother to
the other animals, part of the natural world and competent
to belong in it. . . .*

*We simply need that wild country available to us, even if we
never do more than drive to its edge and look in. For it can be
a means of reassuring ourselves of our sanity as creatures, a
part of the geography of hope.*

THOSE WORDS ARE FROM a letter Wallace Stegner wrote in
1960 to a researcher studying wilderness preservation for the
federal government. A copy of the letter came into the hands
of then Secretary of the Interior Stewart Udall, who interrupted
his own remarks to read it aloud at a conference on wilderness
in San Francisco. The proceedings of the conference were made
into a Sierra Club book, and during the late 1960s a copy of the
book happened into my life. I was eighteen or nineteen, fresh

from the East, trying to be a student at Reed College in Portland.
I skimmed among the book's contents, finding much of interest,
but it was Wallace Stegner's letter-essay, then called "The Wilderness Idea," now called "Wilderness Letter," that took me by
force. I had always been drawn to the outdoors, as a hiker and
fisherman back east, and more recently as a climber. And I had
always been drawn to words and ideas, the sounds of language,
the heft and smells of books. I loved both worlds, but they
seemed almost entirely separate.

Now here was a man writing what clearly was literature—writing with measured passion, with gravity and spirit, with knowledge of history, geography, American authors—and nature, wild
nature, was his very subject. It was big news to me that a writer
could do that. I had read parts of *Walden*, like any high schooler,
but Thoreau and I hadn't connected—because his language
seemed archaic, maybe, or maybe because he was taught in
school. "Wilderness Letter" found me on the loose in the West,
and it showed me that the landscapes I was getting to know had
significance beyond their natural beauty and their service as my
recreational playground. Wallace Stegner made me see that wilderness is all interfused with what it means to be an American.
Wilderness shaped our history, and though we no longer live
in it, it lives in us, as hope and enthusiasm. If we destroy it,
we destroy one of the deep springs of our vitality.

"Wilderness Letter" is one of the great written defenses of
North America's wild nature. Has it changed minds? Today we
have a Wilderness Act and a National Wilderness Preservation
System. Wallace Stegner's conservation writing unquestionably
aided that birth, not by changing minds from one side of the
issue to the other—writing can't do that, not even the best—but
by instilling its passionate reason in the minds of those with similar stirrings, but inarticulate. Wallace Stegner did not change
my mind on wilderness. He formed it. "Wilderness Letter" and
other of his essays gave my thoughts a place to stand, and a light
by which to see.

Years later, when I found the will and discipline to become a writer, his phrases mixed with others in the compost of my reading to give me something else—the beginnings of a style. I liked the way he sounded on the page. I liked the dignity, the authority, the sense he gives of having important things to say and the patience and wherewithal to get them said. The style is formal, but lively with colloquial energy, too. It is personal without being confessional. It points beyond itself to the worthy and enduring things of this world, those of the human realm and those of nature, and values those above its own powers and virtuosity.

The character of the writing, not surprisingly, resembled the character of the man. In 1982 I went to Stanford University, as a poet, on a fellowship bearing Wallace Stegner's name. When the fellowship led to a lecturer's job and I needed a place to live, the director of the creative writing program told me that Wallace and Mary Stegner might have a small house for rent on their property in Los Altos Hills. They did—a redwood-sided cottage, just down the hill from their own house, with a native oak forest on one side and an open field of wild oats and mustard on the other. My wife and I lived there five years, as tenants, as paid helpers around the place, and as friends.

The cottage had once been Wally's writing study. A floor-to-ceiling living room window looked out on the foliage and smooth gray limbs of live oaks—the same oaks, it pleased me to think, that the author of "Wilderness Letter" must have looked upon some two decades before. A hundred-yard trail led from the cottage to our parking area, passing just below the Stegners' deck and Wally's new study. Marilyn and I became accustomed to hearing the steady tap of his Olympia manual typewriter as we walked the trail in the morning. That was his call, and it began as early in the day almost as the birds began theirs. Once in a while a whiff of cigar smoke hung in the air, blending with the scent of bay laurels.

The tall, silver-haired man we began to know was considerate and friendly from the start, but his dignified reticence and my own awed reticence made conversation sparse for a while. I feared that anything of substance I tried to say would betray my considerable dearth of learning, and to make small talk with such a man, unless he began it, seemed disrespectful. Then one morning he put me at ease in a way he couldn't have intended. Walking the trail below his study, I noticed the typewriter was silent. A different noise, a rainlike patter, made me look up, and there was the eminent author, relieving himself over the rail of his deck. It was one of the few times I ever saw him disconcerted, but even then he wasn't much bothered. "Welcome to the country," he said with a grin. "We're not very formal."

I'm told that Wallace Stegner could present a forbidding face in his teaching years, and I believe it, but Marilyn and I saw mostly his smile. It came easily and often to his face, the lines of his age all participating, his eyes lit with equal measures of delight and mischief. I remember him smiling with pleasure at my stepson's talent for soothing a lizard into riding his bare shoulder. I remember him tossing his trowel toward the corner of the yard where he wanted to work next, and grinning to himself when it landed beside the right shrub. And I remember Marilyn talking with a friend, Tanya Berry, about a certain sly sparkle they saw in Wally's eyes. They agreed he was extraordinarily attractive.

"Really," I said. "So he stands out among older men?"

"No, my dear," replied my wife. "He stands out among *men*."

Poised and dignified as Wallace Stegner was, when he smiled you could always see the sensuous little savage, as he called the boy he had been, who started out on the Saskatchewan plains a long time ago. It was in that vast and windy land, with the nearest neighbor four miles away, with the great sky curving clear to the ground in every direction, with mice and coyotes and burrowing owls for brothers, it was there that he first came to a sense of himself as a human being, and it was there that his passion for wilderness first was stirred. Not the idea of wilderness, but the land itself in its wild immensity. In his essay "The Gift of Wilderness" he describes a defining moment that occurred in 1915, when he was six, crossing the empty prairie in a wagon with his father and brother to build a house on their homestead:

Then in the night I awoke, not knowing where I was. Strangeness flowed around me; there was a current of cool air, a whispering, a loom of darkness overhead. In panic I reared up on my elbow and found that I was sleeping beside my brother under the wagon, and that a night wind was breathing across me through the spokes of the wheel. It came from unimaginably far places, across a vast emptiness, below millions of polished stars. And yet its touch was soft, intimate, and reassuring, and my panic went away at once. That wind knew me. I knew it. Every once in a while, sixty-six years after that baptism in space and night and silence, wind across grassland can smell like that to me, as secret, perfumed, and soft, and tell me who I am.

Reading the *Collected Stories* a few years ago, I noticed that nearly half of them are told from a boy's or young man's point of view. Wallace Stegner realized that point of view better than any other writer I know of, and he was capable of that because he and the sensuous little savage never parted. Through all his years and all his words, he gave the boy life in his art, and the boy gave life to him. And through the boy those big windy plains, and the Rockies and the Wasatch Front, the slickrock country of the Colorado Plateau, the Great Basin and the snowy Sierra—through the boy it was the wilderness West that gave Wallace Stegner his indomitable spirit, that energized his prodigious writing career that lasted from the 1930s into the 1990s.

He relished his work, and not only the work in his study. Usually his writing for the day was done by late morning, and most afternoons he devoted to the place, the home on a hill where he and Mary lived for nearly half a century. Together they humanized the foothill landscape in ways that left the wildness in it. Native oaks and planted pines grew up around their pale green house; they built their deck around one of the oaks. They kept their beds and hedges in an easeful kind of order—nothing regimented, nothing cropped in hard lines. Deer and the occasional fox or coyote passed among their shrubs and citrus trees. Wally did make war on gophers, whose insults to the grounds he found insufferable. And he claimed to have knocked off loudmouth jays with his pellet gun, but I didn't believe him.

He would move from task to task around the place, weeding here and fertilizing there, pruning the roses, rooting out a shot lemon tree and planting another, spading a new bed in the impossible dobe soil. There was only a week in the spring and a week in the fall when you could work that soil, he grumped—the rest of the year it was sodden clay or baked brick. At age seventy-seven, the year *Crossing to Safety* came out, he built a tool shed almost single-handedly. "Such as she is, such as she may become . . . ," I heard him intoning one day as he banged nails. Outdoor work seemed to bring out the poetry in him. When I'd pass by on my chores, he'd often have a few lines of Frost or Wordsworth for me. Once I found him declaiming a version of Milton about a gopher he'd trapped. "Which way he flies is hell," sang Wally, unimpaling the rodent and tossing him to the field. "*Himself* is hell, foul vermin. . . ."

There was a particular kind of work he called "idiot's delight"—clipping the leaves off small prunings from the trees, then clipping those twigs and shoots into thin sticks of kindling. Despite his name for it, he enjoyed that work. With the Giants on the radio if they were playing, he'd stand shirtless in the sun and clip his way through an afternoon, turning debris that I would have dumped in the field into fuel that would dry through the months and warm his study on chill winter mornings. When the woodbox was full, he'd start heaps here and there like pack-rat nests. He was a man who took little for granted, who wasted nothing, but idiot's delight told more of him than frugality. It was one of his ways of recharging, of letting the pool replenish. And, I gradually came to see, all that clipping and storing was a novelist's work, a long-timer's work—the work of a man who knew the labors of countless mornings, cold fingers hitting the typewriter keys, the fireplace returning the small saved warmth of days gone by.

He was working on the back terrace one afternoon, pulling up sagging bricks and resetting them in sand, when I came home from teaching and joined him. For several minutes I did more talking than work. It was a bad day and a bad quarter; I was teaching more than I was used to and feeling kind of frazzled. How, I complained, could I finish my manuscript of poems? How could I write new work? I had no time, no energy left over.

Wallace Stegner answered my complaint with the most profound rebuke I have ever received. He spoke as generously as he could. Kneeling to his work, smoothing the sand and carefully setting each brick, he gave me the lasting benefit of his silence. He allowed me to realize, with no word from him, that no word was needed. His example was answer enough—he who had finished *The Big Rock Candy Mountain* snowbound in an underheated Vermont cabin, on unpaid leave from Harvard, writing reviews and what he called potboilers to support his family as he threw himself at the novel seven days a week. No one made time for Wallace Stegner to write. He made it himself, just as he made time to clip twigs into kindling, just as he made time to tap and settle old bricks into sand as carefully as he crafted a paragraph.

There was a way he had of shuffling along in a deliberate kind of hurry, hose or rake or flowerpot in hand, his torso tilted forward, feet keeping close to the ground. It was eager and careful at the same time. Since he died I've been seeing him walk that way, and I've been thinking of all he got done in an afternoon, shuffling from orchids to carport to pool to pyracantha, slipping into his study maybe once for a quick flurry at the typewriter. And I've been thinking of all he got done in a lifetime, too—how he shuffled around the West as a boy, shuffled on through schools and jobs to the work of writing, from Utah and Iowa to Wisconsin and Cambridge, Vermont to California, California to Vermont, Rockies and Great Basin to Los Altos Hills, from word to word, and sentence to sentence, and page to page. Look at all he made, in his slow hurry, by the time he was done.

"You don't go there to find something," he once said about wilderness, "you go there to disappear." Now Wallace Stegner has disappeared into the wildness of the world he loved. Few men and few women will leave more of themselves to the living. Now the writing must stand for the writer—his stone, his witness, his generous bequest. His epitaph might come from any number of his pages. For me it is a passage from the title piece of *The Sound of Mountain Water.* An eleven-year-old from the dryland prairie is standing beside his first mountain river, in the Yellowstone country. A man is looking back to write about the river, and about the boy, and by the time he comes to his final paragraph, he is writing a portrait of his own spirit:

By such a river it is impossible to believe that one will ever be tired or old. Every sense applauds it. Taste it, feel its chill on the teeth: it is purity absolute. Watch its racing current, its steady renewal of force: it is transient and eternal. And listen again to its sounds: get far enough away so that the noise of falling tons of water does not stun the ears, and hear how much is going on underneath—a whole symphony of smaller sounds, hiss and splash and gurgle, the small talk of side channels, the whisper of blown and scattered spray gathering itself and beginning to flow again, secret and irresistible, among the wet rocks.

Sons and
Grandsons
Ed McClanahan

THE DAY AFTER Wallace Stegner died, I was driving home from the Cincinnati airport (after seeing my wife off to Antwerp to look to her dying mother; these things have a way of coming in bunches), when I happened to tune in to an NPR commemorative replay of an interview with him conducted a year or so before his death. In the interview, Mr. Stegner (I was never able to call him Wally, though he asked me to several times) speaks at length, and feelingly, about coming to terms with the memory of his difficult relationship with his long-dead father, which was the principal subject of his great novel, *The Big Rock Candy Mountain*, the book that made him famous. The interview was very moving—like having him in the car with me for half an hour.

I first met Mr. Stegner in the fall of 1962, when I came to Stanford on a Stegner Fellowship in Creative Writing just a couple months after I'd lost my own father, with whom I too had had an uneasy relationship. So I arrived that fall at Stanford, newly fatherless, and there was . . . Mr. Stegner.

He was, at all odds, the handsomest, most urbane, most

instantly certifiable *gentleman* I'd ever encountered—like one
of those "Men of Distinction" gents in the old Calvert Reserve
whiskey ads. I was awestruck. He soon became a sort of spiritual
father to me, first as my teacher in the fiction seminar, then as my
boss when, after my year on the Fellowship was over, he invited
me to stay on as a visiting lecturer in the writing program. Naturally, like any dutiful son, I took it as my filial responsibility to
espouse views and behave in ways which were anathema to him.

But did I say *visiting* lecturer? Hey, I hung onto that job like a
barnacle; it took the English Department nine years to dislodge
me from it.

It was an exhilarating time to be at Stanford. The anti-war
movement and the civil rights movement and the free university
movement and the hippie movement and what we might call, in
retrospect, the General, All-Purpose Up-Yours Movement were
all flourishing, and I was ardently attached to each and every one.

By the mid-sixties, I was industriously insinuating myself into
every sit-in and teach-in and be-in and love-in that happened
along. I was also going around the campus in a knee-length red
velvet cape, accessorized with a mod-bob haircut and granny
glasses and Peter Pan boots. "Captain Kentucky," I styled myself,
while Daniel Boone turned over in his grave.

Now Mr. Stegner was as stoutly in favor of civil rights and as
stoutly opposed to the war in Vietnam as I was, but he strongly
disapproved of the Movement's tactics, which he believed—cor-
rectly, I see now—were detrimental to the university and destructive of rational discourse. Nor was he all that thrilled by—to use
the buzz-phrase of the day—"alternative lifestyles," of which I
was a gorgeously egregious specimen.

Yet throughout the sixties, he not only kept this psychedelic
eyesore on as his aide-de-camp in the writing program, he even
let me share his office! He met my excesses and apostasies not
with stern, authoritarian paternal disapproval, but rather with
unfailing—if somewhat bemused—kindness and unstinting gen-

erosity. In office conversation, he and I often disagreed about political and social issues, but—thanks largely to Mr. Stegner's good nature and forbearance—we never, ever argued.

Part of my job was to read and assess each year's Fellowship applications, and he treated my evaluations of them with courtesy and respect. He took me to lunch at the Faculty Club, and secured me invitations to what I like to call cocklety factail parties. Through him, I met William Styron and Frank O'Connor and Tillie Olsen and Thom Gunn and Gary Snyder and Herb Gold and many other writers.

When CBS television came to Stanford to film an hour-long special on the writing program, he chose me to read my work before the cameras. And when, at the close of the decade, the English Department began endeavoring in earnest to pry me and my anemic bibliography loose from its impenetrable hull, he steadfastly championed my already lost cause to the bitter end. I always had the feeling that he liked me *despite* his better judgment—which I take to be the highest kind of compliment.

That Wallace Stegner was a masterful writer and a great teacher, everybody knows. But for those of us who were blessed to know him personally, I'd venture to say it's his humanity, his dignity, and his generosity that we most sorely miss.

I spent my year on the Stegner Fellowship—the academic year 1962–63—writing a novel about a Kentucky schoolbus driver. It wasn't very good, and it never found a publisher, though I continued to think about it a lot, and to work on it sporadically over the years. I fervently hope it's very much improved for the process, because the novella, now entitled "Finch's Song," will be published this spring, as part of my new book, *A Congress of Wonders*. The original version was about 125 manuscript pages long; the new one is 90 pages long. So I figure that I've *un*written this story over the past thirty-some odd years, at the rate of about one page a year.

But I wrote the original under Mr. Stegner's watchful eye,

and his gentle but astute critique of it all those years ago has been invaluable in helping me to understand what was wrong with the story and how to go about fixing it. I think the fact that it is at last about to be published is a tribute less to my persever-ance than it is to the iron durability of Mr. Stegner's good advice. I only wish he could be on hand to welcome this spanking new 33-year-old "grandchild" of his into the world.

Wallace Stegner (holding dog) and brother Cecil,
Seattle, Washington, 1912.

Wallace Stegner with college friend Dave Freed,
University of Utah tennis team, c.1930.

Wallace Stegner, c.1940.
(Photo: Bachrach)

Wallace Stegner with Mary Stegner and son, Page,
Greensboro, Vermont, c.1942.

Wallace Stegner, as Director of Creative Writing Program
at Stanford University, Stanford, California, c.1947.

Wallace Stegner in Stanford University
Creative Writing seminar, Stanford, California, c.1947.
(Photo: John Lawrence. This photograph originally appeared
in *Mademoiselle*)

Wallace Stegner and Page playing cards
at their campus home, Stanford, California, c.1947.

Wallace Stegner with Mary Stegner and Page at writer
Yasunari Kawabata's home in Kamakura, Japan, 1950.

c.1960.

Wallace Stegner in the Black Rock Desert,
Nevada, c.1960. (Photo: David Miller)

Wallace Stegner (center) with Secretary of the Interior
Stewart Udall (to his left), Mary Stegner (far right),
and National Parks Advisory Board member Sigurd Olson
(far left), c.1961.

Wallace Stegner at the Montgomery House (affiliated
with Dartmouth College) in Hanover, New Hampshire, c.1981.
(Photo: Kelly Wise)

Wallace Stegner in his study at his Los Altos Hills home
in California, c.1980. (Photo: Leo Holub)

Wallace Stegner in the hills behind his home in Los Altos Hills, California, c.1982.

Mary Stegner and Wallace Stegner in Greensboro, Vermont, c.1987.
(Photo: Copyright David Binder, 1996)

Wallace Stegner signing books at Kepler's Books,
Menlo Park, California, c.1990. (Photo: Carolyn Clebsch)

This Challenging and Upright Man

Nancy Packer

I FIRST MET WALLACE STEGNER at a dance thirty years ago. He was already a famous writer, yet as we fox-trotted around the room he was easy and friendly and perfectly willing to take seriously the pompous talk of a young would-be writer.

He was extremely good-looking: slightly graying, those strong Scandinavian features, tall, elegant, broad shoulders. It's such a nice change, isn't it, that men can no longer publicly comment on female pulchritude but women can now talk about male pulchritude.

I was simply bowled over by him. Everyone who knew Wally, women and men, fell at least a little in love with him, and I confess that from then on I have been. But I'm no round heels. I don't fall for every pretty face, although that helps. No: they have to be hard to get, to offer a challenge. Of course I didn't know the challenge was going to last a whole lifetime.

Wally was, in fact, a lifetime challenge not just for me but for Ernie Gaines and Wendell Berry and Scott Turow and Larry McMurtry and Donald Justice and all the writers who

studied at Stanford. He challenged both our talent and our
integrity. His was the respect we sought and his achievement
was the high-water mark we measured ourselves against.
Not only did he inspire the id, but also he constructed
the superego.

This formidable yet dear man was a product of North America's
Great Plains, as indigenous to the West as an old prairie dog. He
spent his boyhood in Saskatchewan. In *Wolf Willow*, he describes
this sparsely settled and forbidding land this way: "winter wheat
heavily headed, scoured and shadowed as if schools of fish move
in it; spring wheat with its young seed-rows as precise as comb-
ings in a boy's wet hair; . . . and grass, the marvelous curly prairie wool tight to the earth's skin, straining the wind as the wheat
does, but in its own way, secretly."

Wally spent a great part of his adult life trying to educate the
American public and our politicians about this national treasure.
He served on the board of the Sierra Club and the Wilderness
Society and founded the Committee for Green Foothills. He
served as a special assistant to Stewart Udall in the Kennedy
administration. And he wrote wonderful books that celebrate
the prairie and the wilderness, books like *Wolf Willow, The Sound
of Mountain Water, American Places* with Page Stegner, and in 1987
The American West as Living Space.

In these wonderful books, he warns us against earth-movers,
extractors and denuders who sacrifice the future for the fast
buck, leaving mining scars a mile wide, destroying the natural
habitat of the owl and the beaver, tearing down redwood forests
to throw up glitzy hotels where people can stay when presum-
ably they come to look at the redwood forests. If Wally had his
way, there wouldn't even be tour buses going through, destroying
the wilderness with their noxious fumes. If you want to see it, get
out and walk.

I don't know if Wally knew this poem by Gerard Manley Hop-

kins—though I'd be surprised if I know something he didn't—
but he might have taken it as a guiding principle:

> *What would the world be, once bereft*
> *Of wet and of wildness? Let them be left,*
> *O let them be left, wildness and wet;*
> *Long live the weeds and the wilderness yet.*

There is a paradox in Wally's prairie. "Puny you may feel,"
he said, but "humble" you are not. He wrote that "You become acutely aware of yourself. The world is very large, the
sky even larger, and you are very small. But also the world is
flat, empty, nearly abstract, and in its flatness you are a challenging upright thing."

We can learn something about this challenging and upright
thing the prairie produces from Wally's books, especially *Big
Rock Candy Mountain*. I don't know exactly which parts of *Big Rock*
are sheer invention and which are transformed recollection. But
the book conveys a time and a life intently and immediately lived
on the prairie.

The father of the family, Bo Mason, is energetic, willful, vola-
tile. He heedlessly drags his family across the West, in search of
the Big Rock Candy Mountain. According to his son Bruce, Bo
Mason was "completely masculine" and an "undeveloped human being." The mother, Else, though she lacks her husband's
talents, is the source of wisdom, sensitivity, and stability.

Bruce, the survivor of the Mason family, might be called a
momma's boy, and it is precisely because he is a momma's boy,
incorporating her virtues and her values into his masculine self,
that he has a chance to be a completely developed human being.

I think Wally's vision of the complete person is androgynous.
He probably would hate my using that term, with its overtones
of academic chic and the effete. But to avoid it, I'd have to use
twenty words and he wouldn't have liked that excess any better.
But he and Virginia Woolf, the high priestess of androgyny, share

the profound insight that masculine self-assertiveness alone will be incomplete and destructive. Virginia Woolf writes that "some collaboration has to take place in the mind between the woman and the man before the act of creation be accomplished." Likewise Wally—this frontiersman with the western macho myth bred in his bones—suggests in *Big Rock* and other books that the complete human being must incorporate what we think of as masculine and what we think of as feminine.

I don't know if Wally thought the difference between the masculine and the feminine is nature or nurture, but he would probably have said there is no way to get back to nature red in tooth and claw so we might as well go from where we are.

It was Wally's sensitivity to and appreciation of the feminine that allowed him to create perhaps the richest and most complex gallery of female characters of any writer of today. From Else to the passionate Sabrina of *Shooting Star*, to the willful writer Susan of *Angle of Repose*, to the unassuming but strong Ruth in *The Spectator Bird*, to the destructively self-assertive, and undeveloped Charity in *Crossing to Safety*. It is a variety of portraits that would please that finest painter of women, Anton Chekhov.

Critics have generally focused on character and theme in discussing Wally's fiction. It has been described as "digging through the surface" of experience, as "concerned with identity," as exploring how "a good person can and should conduct life." Like Chekhov's, Wally's concerns in his fiction are overtly, deliberately, intensely moral.

That sounds reductive and simplistic. But by moral, of course I don't mean that he says don't steal, don't lie, don't commit adultery. Nobody needs to be told that. I mean that Wally's work is concerned with what it means to be human in this complex world and how behavior is, in truth, destiny. In an interview Wally said that for him fiction is "dramatized belief."

From his books we catch glimpses of his beliefs, that freedom must be earned not merely asserted, that ambition must be tempered by restraint, creativity by reason, self-will by self-knowledge, that love requires acceptance not perfection, that forgiveness is a hard virtue to achieve yet essential.

But it was not "dramatized belief" alone that merited a Pulitzer Prize for *Angle of Repose* or a National Book Award for *The Spectator Bird*. It was also Wally's rich and supple style. He is a master of metaphor, unsurpassed in his descriptive powers, an elegant turner of phrase. Perhaps I've quoted sufficiently to make this point, but let me cite one more passage, describing a cattle drive during a raging blizzard on the northern plains:

"There was one afternoon when the whole world was overwhelmed under a white freezing fog, when horses, cattle, clothes, wagon grew a fur of hoar frost. . . . The men worked with tears leaking through swollen and smarting lids. . . . Their skin and lips cracked as crisp as the skin of a fried fish. . . . There was almost always a continuous snake tongue of wind licking out of the north or west."

I remember when I first read that story. It was a July afternoon but when my husband came home and kissed me, I was shocked that his lips and skin weren't freezing cold.

When Wally arrived at Stanford as a professor of English, he had already arrived as a writer. At age thirty-six, he had published five novels and countless stories. Fiction writers as such were hardly welcome in stodgy old English departments in those days: the only good writer was a dead writer. But Wally was also a scholar and had written scholarly books, like *Mormon Country*, and brought out editions of great works. He could do what other English professors could and he could do what they couldn't.

About this time, 1946, a new kind of student came into the universities, hot off the battlefields of the Pacific and Europe, and raring to learn how to write. And no one could teach them better than Wally. But creative writing was not part of the graduate curriculum anywhere in America except Iowa.

Fortunately, Stanford then as now was different. Out here in the wide open spaces, this university was wide open to new ideas. The Stanford English department was chaired by R. F. Jones, who had two essential qualities for our purposes: first, the imagination to let Wally start a creative writing program, and second, a brother who was a Texas oil man. This oil man, Edward H. Jones, also had two essential qualities: first, the imagination to see what a fine contribution he could make to American writing, and second, the money to pay for it.

Thus began this writing program. A year or so later, Richard Scowcroft joined Wally here at Stanford. Dick also was a scholar as well as a fine writer. These two became, as Wally said, the two wheels of the bicycle, a beautifully balanced team, propelling the program for the next twenty-odd years. Together they encouraged, criticized, nursed, cajoled, perhaps browbeat, certainly midwived some of America's finest fiction writers.

One question I'm sure Wally was asked dozens of times is, Can creative writing be taught? I never asked him the question. I knew the answer was yes because he and Dick taught me. They didn't teach me genius, alas, but they taught me craft. They could word an idea or a criticism exactly to fit the student so that we could incorporate it, make it part of our own creative process, and thus take the talent we had, however frail, and craft it into some kind of form.

I turned in a story the second week I was in Wally's class. I don't remember all his criticisms—there were plenty—but I do remember his writing on page 3, "This baby is a long time learning to walk." It was a perfect metaphor crafted just for me: I was seven months pregnant at the time. After that, my stories were off and running in the first paragraph. I didn't want anybody thinking they were slow or stupid.

Wally taught us also by example. He taught us that even the most talented writer must develop the habit of work. He was about the most disciplined person I ever met.

Unfortunately this lesson didn't always take. Some of us used to spend a mighty lot of time sitting around in the creative writing office, our feet on the table, laughing, cracking jokes.

Wally would come in and say something like, "Well, this looks like fun. I think I'll join you for a minute." He would laugh at our jokes and crack some jokes of his own, and then at the fifty-ninth second he would stand up and reach for the door handle and by the end of the allotted minute he was out of there and back at his desk. The rest of us still had our feet on the table.

I want to comment on another achievement of Wally's, in addition to his wonderful books, his environmental contributions, and his creation of the Stanford Writing Program. In a time when only the fear of disease hinders that strangest of oxymorons, casual sex, and fidelity is defined as serial monogamy, in a time when one of our famous novelists is designing new weapons systems for his next battle of the sexes and another writes in order to universalize his own polygamous instincts—in such a time, Wally and Mary had a wonderful marriage of over fifty years.

I'm aware that we don't really know what goes on in somebody else's marriage. We may think our neighbors are blissful but the next time we walk by, the pots and pans are flying through the windows. But I watched this Stegner marriage closely for thirty years. I watched it in real life and, perhaps more revealing, I watched it in Wally's books. What I saw was mutual respect and tenderness, pride in the other and consideration, loyalty and shared interests.

Mary is the musician. She was studying the violin when she and Wally married and continued to play until a shoulder problem interfered. Now she has turned her talent to the piano. She has also been a licensed decorator and an editor. She edited the *O. Henry Prize Stories* for several years and with Wally edited *Great American Short Stories*.

I once asked her if she ever edited Wally's work in progress. Or was it Wally I asked? They were so close that sometimes I confused them.

Anyway, the answer was that Mary read the work, didn't make explicit criticisms, but by the tone of her response and her questions let Wally know what she thought. He revised accordingly. She thus avoided the confrontation that can destroy the writer's confidence—and marriage.

In *The Spectator Bird* Wally says, "The truest vision of life I know is that bird in the Venerable Bede that flutters from the dark into a lighted hall, and after a while flutters out again into the dark. But Ruth is right. It is something—it can be everything—to have found a fellow bird with whom you can sit among the rafters while the drinking and boasting and reciting and fighting go on below; a fellow bird whom you can look after and find bugs and seeds for; one who will patch your bruises and straighten your ruffled feathers and mourn over your hurts when you accidentally fly into something you can't handle."

What a wonderful description of a wonderful marriage.

A Point of View

Lynn Stegner

I KNEW WALLACE STEGNER for ten years; he was my father-in-law, though for me the hyphened suffix eventually lost its meaning. My past had effectively orphaned me, and when one balmy spring afternoon Page, my husband-to-be, and Wally and Mary's only son, took me up to the house in Los Altos Hills for the traditional meet-the-parents evaluation, I felt doubly the import of this first interview. Wally was out on the deck where lunch had been set, wrestling with a new slipcover for an ancient chaise longue. Rarely could he bring himself to throw things away; if there was any evidence of any residual value, he, the ultimate conservator, would make it work, even if it meant having to make annoying accommodations.

He was a splendid looking man, tall and gracefully postured, with white hair, exotic from a distance, like the crest of a rare creature, and a strong face in which unwavering, blue eyes reposed, gazing out speculatively as though always ready—ready to be amused or engaged, ready to learn. On all counts I regarded myself the unlikeliest of candidates. Abandoning his skirmish with the slipcover—it wasn't clear who had got the better of whom—he greeted me easily and warmly, offending neither of us with an immediate and false closeness, nor a formally cautious distance. He was a master—and there was nothing studied or contrived or effortful about it—at the appropriate: the appropriate word or gesture, attitude and response, the appropriate emotional bearing. This came, I believe, of a natural acumen for determining, measuring, and judging the relationships between things—whether causal or circumstantial—and at all times maintaining a balance. Indeed, in every respect, he was a man of exquisite balance. In *Wolf Willow*, referring to the prairie village of his youth and the ways in which that part of the earth had shaped him, he mentions "the way I adjudicate between personal desire and personal responsibility." Herein lay the machinations of that exquisite balance, the source of his decency and dignity; it was not a balance in the literal sense, because Wally's *desire* was to be responsible. He was a kind of natural aristocrat.

The lunch was simple, elegant, the conversation pleasantly comfortable; I did my best to counter all with overeager, overloud impressions of an impressive possible daughter-in-law, which were met with silent, twinkling forgiveness. I had already read most of his books, I was already and irrevocably unworthy, and in the kitchen following lunch I heard myself say with the casual minimalism of someone who regards herself at an enormous disadvantage, "I'm a great fan of your books."

"I hope to be a fan of yours," Wally replied.

It seemed to me then, and still does, that he could not have made a more self-defining quip. Everything—his beliefs, his values, his methods, perhaps even his disposition to affection—was contained in that lambent reply. Standards exist, he meant, larger concerns, a debt to honesty and truth, and none would be forsaken simply to quarter misguided notions of family loyalty. You're young, he meant, you have a lot of work to do, and while I am prepared to encourage you and to hope for the best, there are principles whose measure I will not shorten for anyone.

It was the sort of remark that had the effect of straightening my spine just a little, and yet it was delivered with such palpable kindness and generosity, a smile that enlisted all his features, that I'm convinced I departed that meeting a wee bit taller. And not because in his presence I felt myself to be somehow better; no. In his presence, *because* of his presence, because of the conduct of his life, I *wanted* to be better. I went away expecting more

of myself, though this upsurge of courage or confidence was
merely the counterreflection of Wally's vision: he believed if
we tried and worked and kept at it that we all could be better
—better caretakers of the land, better brothers to each other,
better keepers of the truth, better writers. He believed in belief,
the power of it, and he was not only willing to employ it, but profoundly sensible about what it would require of him and of others. He worked hard. Learning and understanding, achievements
of any sort, were part of a continuum.

I remember one summer afternoon in Vermont walking
from our house over to Mary and Wally's, a five-minute jour-
ney through moss and maples and black spruce that led me to
the base of their hill, grassy about its crown with small ponds of
fern, giving way at its lower margins to saplings, brush, golden-
rod, incipient weed populations. That was where I found Wally
with a pair of clippers in hand.

"What are you doing?" I said.

"I've just cut 374 joe-pye weed," he announced with a kind
of boyish pride.

"You counted them?"

He smiled a Cheshire smile.

I could see that there were at least that many more to cut;
I knew, as he did, that they would *keep* coming up.

This was the way Wally worked: in steady and orderly incre-
ments, aware of the road he had traveled, aware, much more
aware, of the height of the road he—and the rest of us possess-
ing the courage and will—might travel if we dared. And he was
there in the middle of it, striding along, forward-looking, keeping step with the present. Yet history was always with him—his,
the country's, humanity's. He *wanted* to remember; for him remembering was legacy, a legacy of things discovered, perhaps
comprehended, perhaps even reconciled, a legacy of mistakes
not to be made again, paths to avoid—and that legacy he brought
to bear upon the future. The present was simply where the work
got done.

In 1988 Page and I built a log house from three hundred red pine that he and his father had planted as seedlings forty years earlier out on the old farm in North Greensboro, Vermont, where they had made their first summer camp during Wally's years at Harvard. Naturally Wally admired the house—it was a fine and solid house—but it was the idea of it that enchanted him philosophically: "We grew a house," he said on several occasions and with visible delight. Continuity. Past funding the present, informing the future. Found objects. Natural harmony. The builder or author or narrator or conservationist who, with prudence and polish, and mainly with honesty, might make "a clear statement of the lens." These he valued.

Of course, I was terrifically spoiled, having Page, Mary, and Wally as readers, each of whom brought to the task a lifetime of books read, as well as a variance of perspective and taste, and in Page and Wally's case, the practical knowledge belonging to writers who actually write. When Wally read the first two hundred pages of the first draft of my first novel, he wrote me a long and gently pragmatic critique—but the upshot was, I was going to have to start over. I spent two days in a kind of agony of waste—time, hope, effort—pretty handily defeated by the immensity of what I didn't know, and of what I would have to do. I cried a lot. On the third night following receipt of Wally's critique, when we were all in San Francisco for the book-signing celebration of *Crossing to Safety*, Page mentioned my distress to his father; until then, I had concealed it. It was late, we were driving down the peninsula, and Wally and I were in the back seat. He patted my hand, murmured something to the effect that I ought not to be upset, and then went on to discuss point of view—how this was the most important of the early decisions an author must make, how it would shape naturally the course of the story and its telling, and how he felt I ought to confine the point of view to a single character. Which I did. When he read the third draft of the novel, a small, exhilarating infection of faint "ok's" appeared in the margins of the manuscript. He did not dispense praise wantonly; I suppose he felt to do so would be somehow irresponsible. But one "ok" from Wally equaled the effusive paragraphs and exclamation marks of others. The "ok" meant something more, though: it meant *this is fine, perhaps better than fine, but don't settle down here, keep growing.* On the other hand, he felt that recognition was important. One summer I earned second place in a national short story contest. I never mentioned it to Wally and Mary, though at some point Page did.

"Why didn't you tell us?" Wally asked me.

"Oh, well," I fumbled, "by comparison . . . well, it seemed inconsequential."

"It isn't," he said. "It isn't at all." But I could see he was in other ways pleased not only by the temperance, the recognition of a larger, more mature tribe and my apprenticeship in it, but more importantly, by the sense of what there was yet to do, and to try to do. Now I have a second novel coming out and, at least in terms of the progress, I think he would be proud.

As with his writing, he was in life direct and unflinching, reliable as the land he loved. Unless Mary stepped in to whisk him away, or impose a cautioning restraint, he often found himself in the grip of helpfulness. When I was seven months pregnant, summer of '88, the days trailing off behind the weatherman's morning mantra—*hazy, hot, and humid*—six weeks going, and we had a wood floor to lay in the new house, Wally, at age eighty, was there with Page, on his hands and knees, with his bad hip, and the bad heat, singing some work jingle from his youth—all to spare me the toil. He was the original gentleman, without the mannered trappings that might condescend, or make one uncomfortable. Of women he was particularly respectful and cherishing, seemed almost to wince whenever he saw me carrying anything, even a laundry basket, as though, knowing some of what my life had been, he would now wrest from me *any* burdens. When we all went to Italy in 1985 I was seldom allowed to carry suitcases. A tray of champagne glasses I was passing around at *his* birthday party was preemptively snatched from my hands.

And of course for Mary he was a kind of knight. They did everything together, walking, reading, editing, they even baked bread
together, she mixing the ingredients, he popping in from his
study at the requisite intervals to pound and knead the dough.

When Page and I were married in Vermont—a dozen friends,
a short ceremony—it was Wally who took my arm and walked
me in to the house. This gesture was not prearranged or discussed, not assumed by me, not imagined. There was no one
to give me away. But, characteristically, Wally found the sim-
plest, most perfectly lovely gesture with which to officially welcome me into the family.

There were certain kinds of assumptions for which he had little tolerance. One of these was the assumption that there existed
"an easy way," and that one had only to locate it, or finesse it. He
was faithful to whatever bond he made—to a book, to a place, to
a friend, to a woman. He was witty, which is not to say he was
funny: funny is a broader, sloppier thing, and Wally's witticisms
were like small, intricate gifts wrapped in beautiful timing that
went on pleasing the mind as well as the heart long after their
moment of delivery. He sang when he was happy, folk songs of
the Old West; he could play a blade of grass for my daughter's
delight. In the pursuit of daily chores he could find the sublime.
He made connections, often between the seemingly wildly dis-
parate, producing metaphors with prismatic effect. He liked
football, Mozart, my lemon meringue pies. What he didn't like
inspired for the most part his silence, except for the abuse of
Western lands about which he was practically evangelical, I suppose because he believed that something like evangelism was
what it would take to save them. He admired diligence, understatement, the skillful impersonations of the mockingbird
perched on the wire above the house. He admired a willing-
ness to do things on one's own, even while on a larger scale he
believed cooperation was what finally would preserve the land
and improve its civilization, and render humanity a more
humane species.

On any scale and at any distance, maybe especially up close, he was a hero. Truth lies in the details, and from the "small muscle jobs" (as he referred to them), like baking bread or laying floors or cutting down joe-pye weed or tapping out a travel piece, to the large muscle jobs, like trying to save the West from itself, or writing a Pulitzer Prize–winning novel that would embody and enliven western settlement without romance, without the figments of myth, without undue promise, Wally was exactly what he appeared to be, behaved according to what he believed was decent, responsible behavior, and he wrote what his heart knew to be the truth. His life flowed easily into his work, his work was no intruder in his lived life, and between the two he resisted sleights of hand, fabulous optimism, short cuts, language for its own or his own aggrandizement.

Wally never granted himself the stature that others granted him, though he deserved every inch of it. I suppose he didn't want it to get in the way of work there was to do. He was intent on progress, eager about it, and by that I mean the progress of the species. Perhaps he thought that too much self-appreciation would have weakened resolve, or robbed him of the necessary urgency to keep moving forward.

I suppose knowing him, being in his close presence, might have been at times dangerous—to one's own capacity for self-acceptance. Because he was emphatically yet quietly *great*. And gracious, and wise, as good a citizen of a dinner party as he was of this country, a participant, a giver, a human being who genuinely *felt for* others and without a sentimentality that would have had a reductive effect. Of course, he possessed huge gifts, but these gifts would not have attained their full range of consequence had he not at the same time accepted with characteristic humility the obligations they implied and the work they suggested. For he was above all else a tireless, enthusiastic worker.

I suppose one might have felt somehow *less* around Wally but, aside from the fact that *he* never regarded anyone as essentially less (indeed, accorded one and all decorous attention and respect) there was the simple fact of his being, the quality of his being, like a single note struck purely, without distortion, and sounding across the miles and the years with undiminished beauty. His presence was like a call to duty; around Wally I could seldom sit idle.

Around Wally, too, I felt possibilities within and without; what he taught me, among many things, was that to disregard possibilities—both good and bad—was to abandon life. Wally never abandoned life.

I loved him. I told him frequently; it is in my nature to do so. And it always seemed to embarrass him—not the sentiment, but the statement of it. Like the characters in his novels, he was a man revealed through his actions, and his actions were thoroughly and more than sufficiently expressive of deep concern, and of affection carefully tended. He simply preferred evidence to emblems.

Point of view—this, he told me, was one of the most important formative decisions a novelist must make. A man, too, perhaps. It seems to me that early in Wally's life he must have made just this sort of decision, and he stood by it, and it shaped and informed him as a human being. His was a point of view both singular and encompassing. Fortunately, he shared it with the rest of us.

Father, Teacher, Collaborator

Page Stegner

WHEN CHUCK RANKIN WROTE ME last spring to invite me to
this conference I said, without deliberating very seriously about
whether I had anything to contribute, that I would be delighted
to do so if I didn't have to pretend to be scholarly, and if I could
just maunder on anecdotally for a few minutes and sit down.
I think it was the opportunity to hear such distinguished speakers that compelled me, because both before my father's death
and since, I have been asked if I would speak about, or write
something about him, and heretofore I have always refused.
It would have embarrassed us both when he was alive and that
hasn't much changed since his death. And anyway, I don't have
any "daddy dearest" tales to tell; if there are skeletons in the
closet I am unaware of them; and I have never been all that interested in the subject that seems to pique the curiosity of most of
the magazine editors who call—to wit: how tough was it growing up in the shadow of a mountain as big as Wallace Stegner.

Having nothing to compare it to, I don't know how tough it
was. Also, it has occurred to me, when I was growing up, the
mountain wasn't yet that big or the shadow that long. In fact,
at Stanford in the early 1960s I can remember defending the
paterfamilias at a rather drunken English department party by
depositing one of my graduate student colleagues in the chair-
man's fish pond for proffering, through his faux British nose,

the sonorous observation that Wallace Stegner was plainly a minor figure on the American literary scene.

That opinion was clearly in error, then as now, and I imagine a number of the speakers here this weekend will bear witness to the major importance of such books as *The Big Rock Candy Mountain*, *Beyond the Hundredth Meridian*, *Wolf Willow* (which contains the superb novella "Genesis"), *The Gathering of Zion*, and the two collections of short stories, *Women on the Wall* and *The City of the Living*—all of which were written and published well before I deposited my colleague in the fish pond. If there was any question of literary standing in 1964, *All the Little Live Things*, *The Sound of Mountain Water*, *Angle of Repose*, *The Uneasy Chair*, *The Spectator Bird*, *One Way to Spell Man*, and *Crossing to Safety* dispelled them. Among other things.

When I think about lineage and kinship—my own, that is— I do not think of shadows, mountains, or difficulties associated with being the offspring of an increasingly famous father. I think, rather, of being the lucky son of a man who was as devoted to his responsibilities as husband and father as he was to his public reputation, and whose ambitions did not include the pursuit of any literary reputation beyond that generated by the works themselves. I think, too, of having been the lucky son of a consummate teacher, because it has shaped the direction of my own life profoundly, and when I think about him now (as I have been doing for these remarks today) it is in that capacity around which most of my recollections revolve. And by consummate teacher I mean one who was able to share and impart a wealth of knowledge and wisdom to a very recalcitrant student (me) who up until his late twenties didn't think he much needed to learn *anything*. (Of course, as a subadult I knew everything worth knowing.)

My father was a teacher in the most conventional sense: he gave me books to read, endlessly corrected my grammar, gave me *detailed* instructions on the difference between lie and lay, read my school themes and essays and went through them with me laboriously, suggesting changes to both content and structure that might improve their substance and distinctiveness. He was not, I might add, particularly liberal with praise. "Okay," he would say, when I came home from school with five As and a B+, "but still room for improvement." That was about as lavish as it got. Even when I was thirty-five years old with three novels and a critical study of Vladimir Nabokov under my belt he would still write "ok" in the margin of a new manuscript I had given him if he particularly liked something, and type out two pages of thoughtful criticism when he thought something had gone astray. Perfection, or as close as one ever gets to it, comes in the fifteenth or twentieth draft was always his message, and I'm glad I heard it early in my life. I'm sorry so few of the students I've encountered in my own twenty-five-year teaching career didn't have someone like my father come into their room, holding the latest book report between thumb and forefinger as if it were a slightly ripe codfish, and say, "Well, let's sit down and go over this one more time."

But more important, I think, than any formal instruction he offered was his habit of imbuing virtually everything he came across with substance. My father, for example, could never just *look* at scenery. If we happened to be driving across the Colorado Plateau through southern Utah, say from Cisco to Price along the Book Cliffs, he'd offer up an anecdote about Powell being rescued by Bradley in Desolation Canyon, and then explain to his slightly annoyed eight-year-old boy (me), who was trying to concentrate on his Batman comic, who Powell was and why he was important. Then he'd point out the La Sals and Abajos to the south and tell that boy something about laccolithic domes, betting him he couldn't spell laccolithic. He'd comment on the immensity of geological time and the number of Permian seas responsible for the deposition of the Moenkopi, Chinle, Wingate, and Kayenta formations (he could identify them all) on our left and the Dakota sandstone and Mancos shale on our right. He'd observe the Fish Lake Plateau far to the west and remember something of his boyhood summers at that lake, though he was never particularly loquacious about his own childhood except in his writing. Crossing over the Wasatch Plateau and heading south through the Spanish Fork canyon would remind him of the specific dates of the Escalante/Domínguez expedition through the region (September 23, 1776), and that it was exactly fifty years before Jedediah Smith came through following essentially the same route. He had a kind of holistic relationship with the land, and he couldn't look at it without remembering its geological history, its exploration, its social development, its contemporary problems, and its prognosis for the future.

As a boy I always thought I was hearing a lot more about all this than I wanted to know, but in retrospect, I concede I was wrong. In fact, I thought about how wrong I was just two weeks ago when my wife and I were returning from our summer home in Vermont. It was a morning flight, but that didn't keep USAir from showing a movie to its bored passengers, most of whom they seem to think are more interested in Richard Dreyfus's romp through the bedrooms of New York than in what's outside the window. I suppose they're right. Anyway there was an obvious cultural imperative to close the shade during the show.

The movie began somewhere over Illinois—I know because I looked down and recognized the Illinois River where it runs south from Chillicothe to Peoria on its way to the Mississippi above St. Louis. When the movie was over I opened the blinds and looked out, or down—35,000 feet down—and was a bit surprised to discover it took me about thirty seconds to identify exactly where we were. There was the Colorado where it hooks around Moab and creates the only major wetlands on the entire upper stretch of the river, there was Wilson Mesa, the Island in the Sky, the Green River through Labyrinth Canyon. To the south, off the left wing tip, I could see the confluence of the Green and Colorado at the mouth of Cataract Canyon, and farther south still the Henry Mountains, the Circle Cliffs, the Kaparowitz Plateau. I could identify (and did for my long-suffering wife) virtually everything I could see, and it suddenly struck me why this was so, and who had taught me to assimilate the western landscape so completely that I could tell where I was almost anywhere west of the Front Range, even from 35,000 feet in the air. I had a great instructor.

I might add, parenthetically, that I took only one formal class from my father—a large survey of the twentieth-century American novel with about 150 students in it and four teaching assistants. I remember I wrote a term paper on John Steinbeck and got a B+. No doubt there was room for improvement. Okay. I took the midterm and got an A; then took the final exam, for which somehow a numerical grade was assigned, and I scored the second highest mark in the course. My father, naturally, did not want to appear to be playing favorite and gave me a B+ for a final grade. I squawked loudly about this injustice, and he left adjudication of my appeal up to his TAs—who happily overruled him. It made him very uneasy, my being in that class. I know because I came across some notes he was writing just before he died, notes, ironically, for an introduction to a collection of my essays, in which he recalled this incident himself.

"If I had known his intentions [to take the course] I might have steered him away," he said, "for how could I trust myself to judge him fairly? And I would have to judge him; grades are a vital necessity to a graduate student, as much of a necessity as judicial integrity is to a professor. What would I do if he did badly? Protect him? Flunk him?" And farther down the page he observed, "He was faithful in attendance, silent in discussions. His term paper came in on time and was very creditable. He wrote one of the best examinations in a big class. Relieved, I was ready to give him a respectable but not superlative B-plus for the course. My reader protested loudly. 'Come on,' she said, 'he's an A student.' To which I replied, 'How would it look if his *father* gave him an A?' After all, I had spent more than twenty years trying to teach that boy that no matter how well he did, there was always room for improvement. But she insisted so long and vigorously that I finally yielded and gave him an A. But I salved my conscience, and reinforced my lifelong lesson by sticking a minus after it."

My father always liked to point to the flaw that weavers deliberately weave into oriental rugs because they know that only Allah is perfect. It was a gesture that greatly amused him.

In 1977 the editor of the *Atlantic Monthly*, whose name escapes me at the moment, came up with the idea that it would be cute to have Stegner *père et fils* coauthor a special issue of the magazine on the West (I mean the real West, not California or the Pacific Northwest). "Rocky Mountain Country" it was called, and we divided the territory up. My father took Montana, Idaho, and Utah. I took Colorado and Wyoming.

I had written two or three stories for the *Atlantic*, but I had never written a lick of nonfiction prose, other than literary criticism; I had no idea that one could employ many of the devices of the fiction writer in such a composition; I had no investigative skills, did not really even know where to go for information, had no accumulated knowledge, had no time to properly do my homework, was utterly unprepared for such an assignment. I cringe when I think about it. My God, I was ignorant.

My father knew, I'm sure, just how ignorant I was, but I think he regarded this in some way as an opportunity, in the guise of a collaborator, to again teach me something. He patiently indicated the directions we might go, the subjects we might cover, people I might want to talk with, and suggested a few bits of background material I might want to thumb through—like Chittenden's *The American Fur Trade in the Far West*, DeVoto's *Across the Wide Missouri*, David Lavender's *The Rockies*, maybe a little Lewis and Clark, Francis Parkman, John Wesley Powell, maybe take a look at Atwood's *Physiographic Provinces of North America*. Just bedtime reading. Not to worry, he said. In three or four months when we had a draft put together he'd go through it and just sort of clean it up.

I don't know if he really had any idea of what he was in for—

cleaning it up. I do know that when all was said and done I didn't recognize a whole lot of my own sorry prose and half-cocked social commentary in the final product, and although my nose was a bit out of joint at being so massively revised, I learned so much from the examination of his deconstruction (and reconstruction) of my work that I haven't written much of anything else *but* nonfiction essays on the American West ever since. I do remember one part of my narrative that managed to slip through intact in that piece had to do with the Colorado River Compact, with water allocations in the upper and lower basin states, and somehow I managed to reroute the Colorado to drain "into the Gulf of Mexico." There were more than a few astonished letters to the editor. How my father's proofreading eye missed that howler, I'll never know. Only Allah is perfect, I guess.

In 1980 we collaborated again (along with the photographer, Eliot Porter) on a book called *American Places*, and this time I must have gotten it right, or closer to right, because I remember few if any suggested changes to the chapters I wrote and no alterations in my parts of the beginning and concluding chapters that we wrote together.

I don't know what conclusions to draw from all this. As I said at the outset, I planned just to maunder on anecdotally until it was time to sit down, so maybe I don't need conclusions. But I guess I come back to those questions about the accidents of birth that I said didn't interest me much, those "how tough it was" queries, and to my sense, on the contrary, that I have been inordinately blessed and lucky. I didn't mean to be a Pollyanna about it. There were times we didn't get along, and things we disagreed about, but it is symmetry, not dissonance, that strikes my reminiscent ear.

If I had to make metaphor out of collaboration I would make it out of something else my father and I happened to team up on, a different form of collaboration that has nothing to do with students, teachers, fathers, sons, learning, books, or any of the things I've been talking about, but that forms a similar, if more

precise, kind of balance. Fifty years ago I helped my father plant
eight thousand Norway pines on two hundred acres of land we
owned in northern Vermont—land I still own—and about five
years ago I cut down three hundred of those now grown trees,
had them milled out flat on three sides, and built a log house out
of them. When I stand outside it sometimes on a warm summer
evening, and look at it weathering there against its dark background of cedar and spruce, I think, Jeez, this is quite totally
amazing. My old man and I, we *grew* this house. I think it's
about as good a legacy as a human being can ever receive.

Taking Our Turn, or Responsibilities

William Kittredge

I'D LIKE TO DEDICATE MY PARTICIPATION in this evening to my mother, Josephine Kittredge, who died on April 13th of 1995. She was eighty-eight years old, a westerner of Wallace Stegner's generation.

While my mother and Wallace Stegner loved what they loved with vital passion, neither of them had much patience with sentiment. After I'd been writing for a number of years, and not publishing very often, my mother asked if I'd give her something of mine to read. Maybe she thought she could give me some tips. So I gave her one of my more experimental short stories—I don't recall which. There was silence while she made her way through twenty or so typewritten pages.

Then she looked up and smiled.

"What do you think?" I asked.

"I think," she said, "I think I would have thought you would have outgrown this sort of thing." Sounds like the sort of thought Stegner might have had.

My mother and Wallace Stegner would have likely argued about politics. My mother tried hard, for instance, to keep on believing in the Republican party even when some of its recent practitioners and manifestations (tax breaks for the already well-heeled) pretty seriously disgusted her.

But she and Stegner would have agreed, I think, about other important matters. My mother and Wallace Stegner both believed we are defined by, and responsible for, the things we do. She and Stegner both insisted on the prime importance of taking care. In their widely various ways they taught me that I could, while trying to be an artist, also be useful; they taught me to understand that many people, like gardeners and cowhands, are artists in the long run.

My mother and Wallace Stegner grew up in and were to a great degree defined by lives in the rough, chancy American West that's mostly gone now. They were tough and useful in sometimes fierce, hardheaded ways, and we loved them for their strengths; so long as they were around we felt at least partways secure; they would face the heat. They were the best we had, and now they're gone. We're on our own.

If we are many of us artists, of what use is our work?

Our art exists, I think, in its most fundamental form, in our continual search for coherencies to inhabit, stories and selves in which we recognize our best humane and compassionate impulses and act on them in self-defining ways.

To begin with, let's think about these words from the work of Wallace Stegner, from *Big Rock Candy Mountain*:

Things greened beautifully that June. Rains came up out of the southeast, piling up solidly, moving toward them as slowly and surely as the sun moved, and it was fun to watch them come, the three of them standing in the doorway. When they saw the land to the east of them darken under the rain Bo would say, "Well, doesn't look as if it's going to miss us," and they would jump to shut windows and bring things in from yard or clothesline. Then they could stand quietly in the door and watch the good rain come, the front of it like a wall and the wind ahead of it stirring up dust, until it reached them and drenched the bare packed earth of the yard, and the ground smoked under its feet, and darkened, and ran with little streams, and they heard the swish of the rain on roof and ground and in the air.

And these, from the story "Carrion Spring," in *Wolf Willow:*

Three days of chinook had uncovered everything that had been under the snow since November. The yard lay discolored and ugly, gray ashpile, rusted cans, spilled lignite, bones. The clinkers that had given them winter footing to privy and stable lay in raised gray wavers across the mud; the strung lariats they had used for lifelines in blizzardy weather had dried out and sagged to the ground. Muck was knee deep down in the corrals by the sod-roofed stable, the whitewashed logs were yellowed at the corners from dogs lifting their legs against them. Sunken drifts around the hay yard were a reminder of how many times the boys had had to shovel out there to keep the calves from walking into the stacks across the top of them. Across the wan and disheveled yard the willows were bare, and beyond them the floodplain hill was brown. The sky was roiled with gray cloud.

Two experiences, both from Stegner's boyhood in the Cypress Hills of southern Saskatchewan—a complex past that was emotionally his, and because of his art sort of fathomable, one moment running with water and hope, the next deeply two-hearted and deceptive, sublime possibilities and what we've made of them adding up, as they have so often in the American experience, to a beginning run at defining who we are and what we would become.

"They would . . . watch the good rain come . . . the ground smoked under its feet." Those paragraphs echo in me like episodes from my own life. This is probably true for many of us who grew up in the American West. It's a notion that leads me to recall first reading *The Big Rock Candy Mountain.* I like to imagine the childish boy who was me out on the screened-in veranda in front of our house in Warner Valley on a summertime evening with that big book propped up in his lap, listening to the voice and the talk and learning to think about the life I was in the midst of, beginning to imagine my way toward attempts at trying to articulate my own love of the great thunderstorms that came down across our valley.

One reason I like to wonder is because Stegner's paragraphs seem like ideal versions of the ones I wanted to write thirty years ago at Oregon State when I first got the urge—notes that don't attempt much beyond emotional accuracy in rendering still moments when the rain is coming—pure notes that rest so quietly at the center of narrative.

The impulse to understand why we revere such moments, which seem to contain the past and imply the future, is, I think, mostly religious and probably the work we all have to get at in the long run, the real work of understanding what we take to be most valuable in our lives, and in our societies, and why. The rewards of material progress, we have to recognize, are mostly toys.

Stegner is an artist who reminds us of responsibilities to those things we are willing to name as sacred. He reminds us that we must never let ourselves be talked out of our most central purposes. Both Wallace Stegner and my mother told me, the one in his work, the other in the privacy of the room where she died, that I'd better get down to defining those things I hold sacred and taking what measures I can to preserve them. Which means saying what I mean, as directly and unequivocably as I can manage.

The way to work toward cherishing the things we revere is not with the anger and selfish righteousness we hear so much of lately, but with compassion and humility, with great patience and with all the fairness we can muster, with gifts and giving, over and again, and over and again, until it's someone else's turn.

Consider all this an introduction to these words by Wallace Stegner, recorded in 1952, included in a book called *This I Believe*, edited by Walt Wheelock and Edward R. Murrow in that same year and broadcast nationally on February 26, 1953. They are invaluable, and should be reprinted as part of this record.

This I Believe

It is terribly difficult to say honestly, without posing or faking, what one truly and fundamentally believes. Reticence or an itch to make public confession may distort or dramatize what is really there to be said, and public expressions of belief are so closely associated with inspirational activity, and in fact so often stem from someone's desire to buck up the downhearted and raise the general morale, that belief becomes an evangelical matter.

In all honesty, what I believe is neither inspirational nor evangelical. Passionate faith I am suspicious of because it hangs witches and burns heretics, and generally I am more in sympathy with the witches and heretics than with the sectarians who hang and burn them. I fear immoderate zeal, Christian, Moslem, Communist, or whatever, because it restricts the range of human understanding and the wise reconciliation of human differences, and creates an orthodoxy with a sword in its hand.

I cannot say that I am even a sound Christian, though the code of conduct to which I subscribe was preached more eloquently by Jesus Christ than by any other. About God I simply do not know; I don't think I can know.

However far I have missed achieving it, I know that moderation is one of the virtues I most believe in. But I believe as well in a whole catalogue of Christian and classical virtues: in kindness and generosity, in steadfastness and courage and much else. I believe further that good depends not on things but on the use we make of things. Everything potent, from human love to atomic energy, is dangerous; it produces ill about as readily as good; it becomes good only through the control, the discipline, the wisdom with which we use it. Much of this control is social, a thing which laws and institutions and uniforms enforce, but much of it must be personal, and I do not see how we can evade the obligation to take full responsibility for what we individually do. Our reward for self-control and the acceptance of private responsibility is not necessarily money or power. Self-respect and the respect of others are quite enough.

All this is to say that I believe in conscience, not as something implanted by divine act, but as something learned since infancy from tradition and the society which has bred us. The outward forms of virtue will vary greatly from nation to nation. A Chinese scholar of the old school, or an Indian raised on the Vedas and the Bhagavad-Gita has a conscience that will differ from mine. But in the essential outlines of what constitutes human decency we vary amazingly little. The Chinese and the Indian know as well as I do what kindness is, what generosity is, what fortitude is. They can define justice quite as accurately. It is only when they and I are blinded by tribal and denominational narrowness that we insist upon our differences and can recognize goodness only in the robes of our own crowd.

Man is a great enough creature and a great enough enigma to deserve both our pride and our compassion, and engage our fullest sense of mystery. I shall certainly never do as much with my life as I want to, and I shall sometimes fail miserably to live up to my conscience, whose word I do not distrust even when I can't obey it. But I am terribly glad to be alive; and when I have wit enough to think about it, terribly proud to be a man and an American, with all the rights and privileges that those words connote; and most of all I am humble before the responsibilities that are also mine. For no right comes without a responsibility, and being born luckier than most of the world's millions, I am also born more obligated.

In Memoriam

Barry Lopez

I HARDLY KNEW WALLACE STEGNER. We met a few times and exchanged letters, but it would be misleading to say that I knew him any better than any other close and admiring reader of his work.

The first time we met was at his home in Los Altos Hills, and what I particularly remember about that meeting was the way humility and wisdom came together in the man. As a young writer, I very much needed to pay my respects, and he let me do that without trying to cut me off, without trying to deny his own worth—which would have been like telling me I didn't know what I was talking about. In that most concrete way I learned something about how a writer should conduct himself or herself. Over the years I came to greatly admire that quality in him, his behavior as a writer. In our era of celebrities, he would have none of it. In an era of self-promotion he just walked away. In an era of obsession with personal goals, he wanted to know how he could help the community.

Stegner saw a continuum, I think, in which writers were part of the human community, with obligations and responsibilities—which might or might not turn out to have a political expression. A separate continuum linked writers, a more-or-less-loosely knit group of men and women intent on telling stories and feeling various degrees of professionalism and spiritual allegiance toward each other. It was in that context, I believe, that Stegner heard me out that afternoon on his deck in Los Altos Hills.

When I had spoken my piece, he said some kind things about my work and put his hand on my shoulder, as if to convey his feeling that we stood on the same floor together—which was not true but, rather, kind and generous, and one might say constructive, because he was demonstrating a way to share.

Years later I was sitting with the writer Wendell Berry in Wendell's kitchen in Kentucky. We came around to talking about Stegner and I told Wendell some of the things that Wally had written me about my work. And we agreed that he was the only man either of us knew who could pay you a compliment in such a way that you felt you had to continue, and maybe do better, just to live up to the implied expectation.

One of the most astonishing things about this man was reiterated for Wendell and me in that moment—Stegner found, or made time for other people. He encouraged people and assisted them. I think he truly believed the world, or at least the West, could become a better place if people were generous with what they had—if they gave away their time, for example, to a vision larger than any vision they themselves had, or could entirely appreciate. In a way this flew in the face of a tradition of hostility in the West, range wars between settlers and cattlemen a hundred some years ago, and now contention between logging and mining interests and conservationists. Wally was saying: We must find a way to trust in our neighbors, to invest in them.

I don't mean to suggest, either naively or with the admiration for another that distills so readily after death, that Stegner was a flawless man. I have no doubt but that he was human, that he stumbled and fell with the rest of us. And I feel no shred of a need to know the particulars of such things. What I want to know, what I look for as a writer, is what good was a person capable of, how did love flourish around him or her? How did what they do help?

News that a person parted his hair in the wrong place or committed some ordinary indiscretion is no news. The news is: How did a person love? That's the news we're eager to hear. That is what we want to know.

So here is this man whom I knew but slightly, who in our first meeting found a way to say, with such integrity, I love you. And he knew what sort of effect that might have, and he meant for that to happen. And that is admirable. I feel as an American writer a responsibility to imitate, for example, Stegner's scrupulous attention to history; but I also feel an obligation to try to conduct myself, as well as I can, with the same kindness and generosity he showed me that day on his deck.

We are all going to die, of course. And deaths remind us to live our lives fully, to take advantage of every opportunity to love and to be loved. And deaths as large as Stegner's—a first-rate novelist and essayist, a model historian, a man who took citizenship seriously—deaths this large remind us how poorly we often do, meaning to love each other.

I don't know that Wallace Stegner ever meant to teach that particular lesson; it's in our way of life that we often teach best what we're not conscious of, by the example of our lives. But I will always remember this about the man, what he encouraged. It is a good idea to love each other, and to love the earth. It is the only way we can make children. It is the only way we can have a place to abide. And by those two things perpetuate ourselves. No one knows what human destiny is, but surely it must be our hope that it is something good, that it is a striving toward what we call God. And we know that it is love and all that love contains—passion, awe, allegiance, ecstasy, respect, selflessness—that carries us in that direction.

If love is to discover and rediscover life, to encourage and protect it, to marvel at it and serve it, that lesson is scripted on the rock walls of Arnhem Land and Cantabria; it has been passed down in Aramaic and Shona, in Gaelic and Mandarin and Chinook; and it comes round to us again in the memories of *Wolf Willow*, the admiring prose of *Beyond the Hundredth Meridian*, the virtue of *Crossing to Safety*. It is the best we can do for each other, to remember, to say it all again. And in this instance of Wallace Stegner, the best he could do was very much enough.

Everywhere
in the
West

Gretel Ehrlich

I DIDN'T KNOW WALLACE STEGNER PERSONALLY, and yet I felt as if I did. His presence was everywhere in the West, and whatever hard-luck sheep camp I was in, or widow-maker horse I was on, I felt he was somewhere, laughing or crying or whatever. I had a lending library at my ranch in northern Wyoming, because there were no libraries very nearby. Easterners always seem to think that westerners don't read, but I found quite the opposite to be true. Stegner's books *Angle of Repose, Mormon Country, Wolf Willow* and all his others made continual rounds of sheep camps, cow camps, and geology camps and went from ranch to ranch all the years I lived there. His histories, novels, memoirs, essays were always in circulation, the way his presence as a celebrant of the West, with all its harshness, grandeur, and human-inspired flaws, circulated among all of us, especially those of us who dared to write about the West, the people and the place. Stegner understood what it was to be a westerner; what it was to be a hick, and also a struggling writer. The little piece that he wrote in a book called *Montana Spaces* I just love. It's such a perfect description of childhood. He wrote:

When my family came down out of Saskatchewan to Great Falls Montana in the fall of 1920 I was eleven years old. For most of my conscious life I had known only our scruffy little village. . . .

I had always been sickly, with croups and coughs and pneumonias, and in winter lived on Scott's Emulsion, a repulsive form of cod liver oil. But I had also lived a life so free and unsupervised that it astonishes me now to remember it. I was much outdoors, both summer and winter. I had owned and used guns since the age of seven or eight, and like frontier boys in general I had grown up killing things—gophers, rabbits, small fur-bearers, even the occasional feral cat whose pelt was worth fifty cents in the St. Louis fur market. And I had secrets darker than I would ever have turned loose. My father's erratic and sometimes unlawful activities had taught me to keep my mouth shut, and given me, along with some private shame, a wariness older than my years. In other ways I was younger, even infantile. And I was studious, a reader, in love with words. When under strain, or when things weren't going well, I sometimes reverted to baby talk that drove my father crazy.

In short, an uncouth sensitive little savage with terminal sniffles, a crybaby with an extensive history of dealing death, a pint-sized loner with big daydreams, clammy self-doubts, and an ego out of proportion to the rest of him.

And ignorant—utterly, wonderfully ignorant.

I think that describes all of us pretty well. Lao Tzu said, "He who loves the world as his body may be trusted with the empire." Now I wish Stegner were our president.

I did something which I've never done before, but I want to have it with me even when I'm traveling to far places as I am tomorrow. I tore a page out of a book, so I could carry it with me. It is part of the wilderness letter that Page referred to. I'm going to read a little bit more, a different section:

Something will have gone out of us as a people if we ever let the remaining wilderness be destroyed; if we permit the last virgin forests to be turned into comic books and plastic cigarette cases; if we drive the few remaining members of the wild species into zoos or to extinction; if we pollute the last clear air and dirty the last clean streams and push our paved roads through the last of the silence, so that never again will Americans be free in their own country from the noise, the exhausts, the stinks of human and automotive waste. And so that never again can we have the chance to see ourselves single, separate, vertical, and individual in the world, part of the environment of trees and rocks and soil, brother to the other animals, part of the natural world and competent to belong in it. Without any remaining wilderness we are committed wholly, without chance for even momentary reflection and rest, to a headlong drive into our technological termite life, the Brave New World of a completely man-controlled environment. We need wilderness preserved as much of it as is left and as many kinds—because it was the challenge against which our character as a people was formed. The reminder and the reassurance that it is still there is good for our spiritual health, even if we never once in ten years set foot in it. It is good for us when we are young, because of the incomparable sanity it can bring briefly, as vacation and rest, into our insane lives. It is important to us when we are old simply because it is there—important, that is, simply as idea.

We are a wild species, as Darwin pointed out. Nobody ever tamed or domesticated or scientifically bred us. [Except, till now.] *But for at least three millennia we have been engaged in a cumulative and ambitious race to modify and gain control of our environment, and in the process we have come close to domesticating ourselves. Not many people are likely, any more, to look upon what we call "progress" as an unmixed blessing. Just as surely as it has brought us increased comfort and more material goods, it has brought us spiritual losses, and it threatens now to become the Frankenstein that will destroy us. One means of sanity is to retain a hold on the natural world, to remain, insofar as we can, good animals. Americans still have that chance, more than many peoples; for while we were demonstrating ourselves the most efficient and ruthless environment-busters in history, and slashing and burning and cutting our way through a wilderness continent, the wilderness was working on us. It remains in us as surely as Indian names remain on the land. If the abstract dream of human liberty and human dignity became, in America, something more than an abstract dream, mark it down at least partially to the fact that we were in subtle ways subdued by what we conquered.*

The man we're honoring describes the West as "a place whose silence is such that you can hear the swish of falling stars." This is his geography of hope. Let's make it ours.

West of the Hudson, Pronounced "Wallace"

Ivan Doig

IF I COULD EVER STAND ON a passing comet and watch the clock of earth below, a moment I would choose is in the summer of 1921. A boxy, spoked-wheel vehicle called a Hudson Super Six is trying to make time on the indifferent dirt road down through the Smith River Valley of Montana. There in the middle of not much but sagebrush, that car passes a rickety small dairy farm called Moss Agate, and the twelve-year-old boy named Wallace there in the carload of the Stegner family heading for Salt Lake City and yet another new try at life, crosses paths—for an instant—with the asthmatic eight-year-old girl there at Moss Agate who will live long enough to become my mother, and a stout, much-put-upon, durable ranchwoman who became my grandmother and ultimately the woman who raised me.

Destinies, outlined against the basic earth. That is the story we all write in the American West, whether in memory or on the white canyons of paper.

In time to come—indeed, in *Times* to come, for this occurred in the pages of the *New York Times*—I suppose I began my own crossing of professional paths with Wallace Stegner when the *Sunday Magazine* editors whomped together a bunch of us they chose to call "Writers of the Purple Sage." Most of us were forty-something then, and a few (no longer including me) even did live somewhere around sagebrush, but the exception on both counts was pictured in distinguished gray-haired presiding manner beneath a California oak and presented to the *New York Times* readership in big hey-look-who-we've-discovered typeface as:

William Stegner.

West of the Hudson River, of course, that first name has always been pronounced "Wallace."

But at least they got it right, back there, that W. Stegner, Pulitzer Prize novelist, National Book Award novelist, and essayist and conservationist and historian and teacher and consummate citizen of the West, was the dean of our congregation.

Wolf Willow. The Sound of Mountain Water. Angle of Repose. The Spectator Bird. Crossing to Safety. Where the Bluebird Sings to the Lemonade Springs. . . . The man could not even write book titles without making music. As did his letters:

"Salt Lake next Tuesday for a speech, and then we can escape to Vermont, which from here looks like a cool green sanctuary. Ah, wilderness. There is too much frenzy and noise around here. Give me my scallop shell of quiet / My staff of faith to lean upon. And nine bean rows. See you in December, I hope."

We did not see each other in December, nor nearly as many other times as I now wish. Yet I will always feel about Wallace Stegner that there was a general benefit to me just being in his region of the country and his line of work.

In person, Wally of course looked like a one-man Mount Rushmore. And his solidity, that Scandinavian-Iowan-Saskatchewan-Montana-Utah-etcetera mien of flat-footed common sense and endurance, went much more than skin-deep. Wallace Stegner knew his stuff, and he knew that he knew it. An academic interviewer once tried to get him to pontificate on "what it is that Western writers will have to do to produce a crop of distinguished novels." Stegner looked at him and said dryly:

"Write good books."

He practiced what he preached, there too, and off the Stegner shelf of about thirty books, let me pluck just one—I think, the smallest one—as a particular favorite. *The American West as Living Space* began as a trio of lectures he delivered at the University of Michigan in 1986, and to me it is a diamond-hard distillation of what Wallace Stegner spent a lifetime of words on. Here's his opening paragraph:

The West is a region of extraordinary variety within its abiding unity, and of an iron immutability beneath its surface of change. The most splendid part of the American habitat, it is also the most fragile. It has been misinterpreted and mistreated because, coming to it from earlier frontiers where conditions were not unlike those of northern Europe, Anglo-Americans found it different, daunting, exhilarating, dangerous, and unpredictable, and entered it carrying habits that were often inappropriate and expectations that were surely excessive. The dreams they brought to it were recognizable American dreams —a new chance, a little gray home in the West, adventure, danger, bonanza, total freedom from constraint and law and obligation, the Big Rock Candy Mountain, the New Jerusalem. Those dreams had often paid off in parts of America settled earlier, and they paid off for some in the West. For the majority, no. The West has had a way of warping well-carpentered habits, and raising the grain on exposed dreams.

Lots of lessons in that one paragraph, an impressive number of them about the art of writing. Parallel constructions, alliteration, deft change of sentence rhythm from that forty-worder which crescendoes in "the Big Rock Candy Mountain, the New Jerusalem" down to the honest power of that four-word dreambreaker: "For the majority, no." More vitally, though, he sweeps us at once into his exploration of the great theme of the West, the clash of its ecologies and its cultures.

In trying to review Wally's last book, *Where the Bluebird Sings to the Lemonade Springs*, I swiped from the Greek poet Archelaus and the philosopher Isaiah Berlin the notion that strong writers, the enduring hedgehog type, are said to know one big thing. Wallace Stegner powerfully always knew his:

"I really only want to say that we may love a place and still be dangerous to it."

He and his irrefutable voice for the land provoked the right enemies. Ronald Reagan saw fit to bestow the Presidential Medal of Freedom on Frank Sinatra and Whittaker Chambers, but not on the most distinguished voice for the natural glory of his own California. Nor did the Jefferson Award, the National Endowment for the Humanities distinguished-career recognition, ever find its way to this most obvious candidate—nominated time and again from the West—during the NEH regimes of Lynn Cheney and William Bennett.

In such telling echoes, Wallace Stegner's was a voice that goes back far—certainly to the spirit of Theodore Roosevelt's words, "I hate a man who skins the land," although I doubt that Wally himself ever used the word "hate." Born as he was in 1909, he was thus a witness to every haywire development in the American West since then, and yet he managed to maintain an almost preternatural patience with his fellow humanity. "The West . . . is the native home of hope," one of his most memorable sentences sang. So say we all, in his spirit.

None of us is going to replace him, and it's just about as doubtful whether any half-dozen writers and thinkers can produce a combined rainbow of work to equal his.

So, in the West, this ever-old, ever-new part of the American land, we resort to the lessons that shaped Wallace Stegner and that he wrote so long and eloquently about. Go on with what you've got. Remember that humanity is a tough neighborhood, and love it nonetheless.

Our advantage is that we have his lifework to draw on, and my hope—here in this honored company of wordsmiths, representing as we do many other writers at this end of the country—my hope is that we can find a paradoxical strength in this loss of him. That instead of Wallace Stegner's long-familiar and often lonely eloquence for the West and its earth, the rest of the country will now have to hear from us as a tribe of western writers. A swarm of us.

In his last years, when the national bestsellerdom of *Crossing to Safety* and his *Collected Stories* inspired paperback publishers to pour his earlier books back onto the bookstore shelves, Wallace Stegner was a bit bemused at getting mined as a new literary resource.

"I'm a land of opportunity," he laughed, "just like the West." Was he ever.

Chronology

Nancy Colberg

1909	Born February 18, 1909, at Lake Mills, Iowa, son of George H. and Hilda (Paulson) Stegner.
1910–14	Family moved frequently—in Iowa, North Dakota, and Washington State.
1914–20	Lived in East End, Saskatchewan, a tiny village on remote plains. Attended grammar school.
1920–21	Fifteen months in Great Falls, Montana.
1921	Moved to Salt Lake City, Utah, where the family lived in a dozen houses over the next ten years. Attended junior high and high school.
1927	Graduated from high school and entered the University of Utah at age sixteen. Was encouraged to write by his freshman English teacher, the novelist Vardis Fisher.
1930	Received a B.A. from the University of Utah and began graduate work in English literature at the University of Iowa.
1932	Completed his master's thesis, which consisted of several short stories, and received an M.A. from the University of Iowa. As a graduate student he began teaching.

1932–33   Began doctoral work at the University of California at Berkeley.

1933   Left Berkeley because of his mother's illness. After her death that year he returned in February 1934 to Iowa to work on his doctorate.

1934   Married a fellow graduate student, Mary Stuart Page, September 1, 1934, and accepted a teaching position at the University of Utah (1934–37). Received his first full-time teaching position at Augustana College in Rock Island, Illinois (a one-semester stint).

1935   Completed requirements for the Ph.D. in English with a dissertation on the Utah naturalist Clarence Dutton (later published as *Clarence Dutton: An Appraisal*).

1937   He and his wife became the parents of a son, Stuart Page, their only child. Achieved national success as a writer when *Remembering Laughter* was published after winning the $2500 Little, Brown novelette prize. Began teaching at the University of Wisconsin (1937–39).

1938   *The Potter's House.*

1938   Joined the staff of the Bread Loaf Writers' Conference, where he formed friendships with Robert Frost and Bernard DeVoto. Began teaching in the writing program at Harvard (1939–45).

1940   *On a Darkling Plain.*

1941   *Fire and Ice.*

1942   *Mormon Country.*

1943   *The Big Rock Candy Mountain.*

1945   Shared the Anisfield-Wolfe Award and received the
        Houghton Mifflin Life-in-America Award for *One Nation.*
        Appointed Professor of English, Stanford University.
        Directed the eminently successful writing program at
        Stanford University (1945–71).

1947   *Second Growth.*

1950   First Prize O. Henry Memorial Short Story Award for
        "The Blue-Winged Teal." (Also received O. Henry Awards
        in 1942 and 1954.) Published *The Preacher and the Slave* and
        The Women on the Wall.

1950–51 Rockefeller fellowship to conduct seminars with writers
        throughout the Far East.

1951   *The Writer in America.*

1954   *Beyond the Hundredth Meridian.*

1955   *This Is Dinosaur* (editor).

1956   *The City of the Living.*

1960   Wrote the famous "Wilderness Letter."

1961   Assistant to the secretary of the interior. Published
        A Shooting Star.

1962   *Wolf Willow.*

1962–66 Served as a member of the National Parks advisory board.

1964   *The Gathering of Zion.*

1967   *All the Little Live Things.*

1969   *The Sound of Mountain Water.*

1971   Retired from Stanford as Jackson E. Reynolds Professor of
            Humanities. Published *Angle of Repose.*

1972   Pulitzer Prize for Fiction for *Angle of Repose.*

1974   *The Uneasy Chair.*

1975   *The Letters of Bernard DeVoto.*

1976   *The Spectator Bird.*

1977   National Book Award for Fiction for *The Spectator Bird.*

1979   *Recapitulation.*

1980   First recipient of the Robert Kirsh Award for Life
            Achievement *(Los Angeles Times).*

1981   *American Places* (with Page Stegner and Eliot Porter).

1982   *One Way to Spell Man.*

1987   *Crossing to Safety. The American West as Living Space.*

1990   *Collected Stories of Wallace Stegner.*

1991   Governor's Award for the Arts from the California Arts
            Council.

1992   *Where the Bluebird Sings to the Lemonade Springs.* Refused
            National Medal for the Arts Award in protest over controls
            imposed on the National Endowment for the Arts during
            the Bush administration.

1993   Cyril Magnin Award for Outstanding Achievement in the
            Arts. Bay Area Booksellers' Award.

1993   Died on April 13 in Santa Fe, New Mexico, from injuries
            sustained in an automobile accident.

Contributors

The Honorable BRUCE BABBITT is a third-generation Arizonan who has written extensively on the cultural history of the Southwest. He was elected Attorney General of Arizona in 1974 and Governor in 1978. He is currently Secretary of the Interior in the Clinton administration.

JACKSON J. BENSON teaches modern American literature at San Diego State University and has won the PEN-West U.S.A. award for nonfiction for *The True Adventures of John Steinbeck, Writer.* He is the author of nine books. His biography of Wallace Stegner will be published in 1996.

WENDELL BERRY'S most recent book is *Another Turn of the Crank.* He is the author of several books, including *The Unsettling of America, The Gift of Good Land,* and *What Are People For?* He farms and lives in Port Royal, Kentucky.

Congressman DAVID E. BONIOR represents Michigan's 10th Congressional District. Since coming to Congress in 1976, Bonior has earned a reputation as a strong voice for environmental issues and encourages interest in the environment by organizing volunteers to distribute pine seedlings in his district.

NANCY COLBERG is a working librarian as well as a book collector and bookseller. She is author of *Wallace Stegner: A Descriptive Bibliography,* published by Confluence Press, Inc., in 1990.

JOHN DANIEL is poetry editor of *Wilderness* magazine and the author of two books of poems. His most recent book is *The Trail Home,* a collection of his essays on nature. In 1982 he received a

Wallace Stegner Fellowship in Poetry at Stanford University and in 1994 he won the John Burroughs Award for Outstanding Natural History Essay.

Born in Montana, IVAN DOIG has worked as a ranch hand, newspaperman, magazine editor and writer, and holds a Ph.D. in American western history. He is the author of four works of fiction and three of nonfiction. He currently lives in Seattle, Washington. His latest novel is *Bucking the Sun*.

GRETEL EHRLICH was born in Santa Barbara, California, and in 1976 moved to Wyoming, where she lived and worked on sheep and cattle ranches for seventeen years. She now divides her time between Wyoming and the central coast of California. Her books include *The Solace of Open Spaces, Drinking Dry Clouds,* and *A Match to the Heart*.

JAMES R. HEPWORTH wrote the first general entry on Wallace Stegner for an encyclopedia and has published essays about and interviews with Wallace Stegner in a variety of periodicals. Hepworth is the co-author of two recent books, *The Stories That Shape Us* and *Resist Much, Obey Little: Some Notes on Edward Abbey*. He is professor of English and publisher of Confluence Press at Lewis-Clark State College in Lewiston, Idaho.

JAMES D. HOUSTON's honors include a Wallace Stegner Fellowship and a 1995 Rockefeller Foundation residency at Bellagio, Italy. He is author of the award-winning *Californians: Searching for the Golden State* and co-wrote with his wife, Jeanne Wakatsuki Houston, the book and teleplay *Farewell to Manzanar*.

WILLIAM KITTREDGE grew up on a ranch in southeastern Oregon and farmed there until 1967. Since 1969 he has taught Creative Writing at the University of Montana. He has published two books of stories, a book of essays, a memoir, and has a forthcoming book, *Who Owns the West*.

PATRICIA NELSON LIMERICK is a professor of history at the University of Colorado. She is the author of numerous essays and books, including *Desert Passage* and *The Legacy of Conquest.*

BARRY LOPEZ is the author of *Arctic Dreams,* several story collections, including his most recent, *Field Notes,* and a collection of essays, *Crossing Open Ground.* He is the recipient of a National Book Award and other honors.

ED MCCLANAHAN is the author of *Famous People I Have Known, A Natural Man,* and *A Congress of Wonders.* He is one of a number of Kentucky writers who held Stegner Fellowships at Stanford during the 1950s and 1960s.

NANCY PACKER taught in the Creative Writing Program at Stanford until she retired in 1993. Her publications include three volumes of short fiction and several textbooks. Her fiction has received awards from the O. Henry Memorial Award Prize Stories and the National Endowment for the Arts.

ARTHUR SCHLESINGER, JR., won the Pulitzer Prize for Biography for *A Thousand Days: John F. Kennedy in the White House.* He is the recipient of many awards and honors and sits on the Advisory Board of the Arthur and Elizabeth Schlesinger Library on the History of Women in America, named in honor of his parents.

GRETCHEN HOLSTEIN SCHOFF received a Distinguished Teaching Award from the University of Wisconsin-Madison, served on the Madison faculties of the Institute for Environmental Studies, the Integrated Liberal Studies Program, and the College of Engineering. She died in Madison on July 10, 1994.

LYNN STEGNER is the author of two novels, *Undertow* and *Fata Morgana.* She teaches part-time in the Creative Writing Program at the University of California, Santa Cruz. She has been the recipient of a Bread Loaf Fellowship, California Arts Council Fellowship, and a short fiction award from The Writers' Workshop.

PAGE STEGNER is Professor Emeritus at the University of California, Santa Cruz. He is the author of two volumes of literary criticism, three novels, and four works of nonfiction. His most recent book is *Grand Canyon: The Great Abyss.*

Since 1982 T. H. WATKINS has been the editor of *Wilderness,* the quarterly magazine of The Wilderness Society. He is the author of twenty-five books. His 1990 biography of FDR's Interior Secretary, *Righteous Pilgrim,* won the Los Angeles Times Book Award. His most recent book is *Stone Time: Southern Utah, a Portrait and a Meditation.*

A graduate of Stanford Law School and former attorney with the Native American Rights Fund, CHARLES WILKINSON is the Moses Lasky Professor of Law at the University of Colorado. His most recent books are *The Eagle Bird: Mapping a New West* and *Crossing the Next Meridian: Land, Water, and the Future of the West.*

TERRY TEMPEST WILLIAMS, author of *Refuge, An Unspoken Hunger, Desert Quartet,* and other works, is naturalist-in-residence at the Utah Museum of Natural History in Salt Lake City. She is the recipient of a Lannan Fellowship in creative nonfiction and in 1995 she was identified by the *Utne Reader* as a "visionary . . . who could change your life."